WARNING!

WAR'S COMING.

Time O. Day

To the son of that Jewish carpenter
who saw me more than a tile man.
And to my mom, Grace,
who was never afraid to thank the Lord.

Contents

WHAT ARE THE ODDS?

On a January night, 1985, in a remote region along the British Colombia coast, a plane dropped into a snow storm.

At that time we didn't know the pilot was battling for his life. From our boat, we simply heard his jet engine. Yes, it was odd that it was flying in that cold blooded snow storm, and unusually close, but that coastline is a point of travel for planes heading for Seattle, Alaska, Vancouver, Prince Rupert, or Terrace.

On that trip we'd been commercial prawn fishing for two weeks, had worked our way up Gardner Channel, and were anchored in Chief Mathews Bay. The four of us were out on deck, under the lights, boxing prawns when we heard the jet. I'm guessing it was close, maybe a mile or two up there. But the falling snow was too dense to see him or see anything but snow.

This event instantly became weirder when we heard the jet coming around again.

Davey, the youngest, 18, stopped stacking tiger prawns in his 8 inch box, and gazed into the blinding snow. "Man, I'm glad I'm down here instead of up there."

"No kidding." I peered into the foreboding whiteout. "That guy's got no business being up there."

At the stern of The Four Seasons, we were sheltered

below an aluminum roof which wasn't more than a sloped awning. Though it protected us from the snow, it was open on all sides, allowing us to clearly hear the besieged jet.

"I wonder if he's picking up our radar?" Tony nudged his wool cap with the back of his hand and joked, "Maybe he's picking up the antennas in my head." This Portuguese kid was near as young as Davey and a lot of fun, but sometimes joked too much.

Paul, the oldest, a wiry fellow in his thirties, looked above the wheelhouse at our circling radar and added, "Maybe he thinks we're an airport or something."

Concerned and itching to see this plane, I shuffled and slid over the slippery deck, opened the door to the wheelhouse, and stepped down. At that time of night the cabin was always lit as we were constantly going in to warm up our fingers at the stove. The wheelhouse wasn't a big affair; the portside held a diesel stove, cabinets, the helm, and radios hung from the ceiling, while other electronics were positioned below the base of the forward windows, our depth sounders and radar. On the starboard side sat a table with a wraparound sitting booth, behind it the galley impatiently waited to cook our meals. Overall, The Four Seasons was a fifty-foot freezer boat that had a long line drum on it. Though it was not that big in commercial fishing standards, I'd never imagined having a boat like that before I was thirty.

Curious to see if I could spot the plane on the radar, I leaned over, put my face up against a rubber grommet that outlined my eyes and stared at the screen. A glowing green bar cut through a dark screen, scanning in a circle, displaying the bay, but I saw no dot on the screen that would identify an aircraft. However, I didn't know if that radar machine was capable of picking up aircraft.

That coastal area was 2nd in the world for most amount of snowfall in the shortest amount of time – Onion Lake had 47" in 24 hours. The snow was coming down so hard and heavy that the bay's water was checking, whiting up like a slushy.

Flipping off the radar, I stepped out on deck to listen. A minute passed before I thought I saw a flash of light up the mountain. This wave was so slight and brief that I dismissed it as my imagination, there was too much snow. As I stared into the whiteout, I was a bit anxious for the pilot, but I held those feelings at arm's length because I hadn't seen the plane and wasn't convinced he was in trouble. Bottom line, the situation was too unreal. True, I'd heard the sound of the jet flying around up there, and knew those mountains were nothing to fool with, rising right out of the sea, powering up to 5,500 feet within a mile, but I never saw the aircraft.

Stepping back inside, I turned on the radios. Though I had a radio license, I didn't use mine enough to be that familiar with, but flipped the dial to a certain channel that the pilot might use for a mayday. The radio silence wasn't unexpected as it was no mystery that he had his hands full in that storm.

Going back outside, I shuffled and slid across the snow covered deck, rejoining the guys who were boxing prawns.

Glancing at Paul, I asked, "Did you hear that plane again?"

"It's gone."

"I didn't see it on the radar."

"It'd be difficult to see on that radar anyway. What would you see? A little dot?"

"That jet's gone." Tony stated.

"It sounded like a small jet, maybe a fighter jet," Davey said.

Paul added, "I bet it came from that interceptor station on Masset."

Masset was on the northern point of Queen Charlotte Island, some three hundred miles to the west of us.

"I didn't know they had an Air Force base?"

"It's part of NORAD, a buddy of mine worked on a renovation there." Paul had a tendency of getting quite serious when he embellished things, his voice very certain. "They're putting millions into it. It's all top secret. I bet there were more fighter jets traveling with this one."

Tony joked, "Maybe they're practicing, flying in the snow."

Davey chuckled, "Shut up, Tony."

It wasn't long before we wrapped up. We never had dinner until after putting the boxes of prawns down on the freezer plates, so we generally ate between 9 and 10 pm.

Around the table that night, I don't recall any dramatic dialog about the plane. It was an unusual event, yes, but we didn't see the plane or hear a crash. Besides, at that time of night, our focus was on eating and the more you talked, the less you got. If one of us felt playful, I should say if Tony felt playful, attempting to game one of us, he might toss a question out to see if anyone would take the bait and give further details, again, giving him more opportunity to eat the talker's portion.

We might answer, "Sure," or "Okay," but we never expounded while we ate. All and all, questions around the dinner table were a standing joke.

Sometimes Tony would break into a small chuckle while eating. I figured he was amused by the visuals of us chomping down, like a pack of hungry dogs.

Maybe it was the elements and the energy spent in going through the motions, dampness especially will suck your power, but I always remember being so starved come dinner that when food hit the table we just got after it. To be frank, when we started eating, it didn't matter if a mermaid were trying to get on board and calling for help; we weren't going to be dealing with her till after we finished eating.

I don't recall talking about the plane after supper either; we'd been working since 6am, and been together, night and day, for two weeks.

We didn't have to get after sleep, she got us. Even with the noise of our diesel engine right behind the mahogany wall, blazing all night to keep our freezer cold, it never hampered our snores. When I fell asleep, that jet engine was a distant memory.

Interestingly, I found out later that the interceptor station at Masset wasn't even an Air Force Base but when NORAD, and top secret stuff was talked about, people had a tendency to exaggerate.

The following morning, I wasn't surprised to see seventeen inches of snow on the decks, but I was surprised to see seven inches blanketing the surface of the entire bay. I'd never seen that before, but freaks of nature in the North weren't uncommon. Chief Mathews Bay is a cuddly little affair, not over a mile long. Our prawn traps were about 30 inches round with nylon mesh encompassing and weighed less than 6 lbs, so when we laid them atop the snow they just sat there, unable to sink. It was comical to see that line draped across the snow to another trap then another trap.

"It looks like we're trapping beaver." Tony gave me a goofy grin. "Have you ever . . ." he started chuckling so hard he didn't finish his question.

Half the time I had no idea what that kid was so jolly

about. Maybe he'd gotten too much fresh air, that's all I could figure.

To speed the trap's downward journey, we ended up using all our concrete blocks. At last gravity prevailed and the sinking traps pulled the reluctant ones under.

As the day wore on, the snow in the bay melted. All that was left were some iceberg looking patches.

Being so far north, in January it gets dark around 3:45 and blacks out by 4:00 pm.. Tony and I were on The Four Seasons on one side of the bay while Paul and Davey were dropping their last line off The Little Mule, (our 30 ft. converted aluminum herring punt with pontoons, a flat top, drum and wheelhouse) on the other side of the bay.

Not long after darkness had fallen, I saw a flare go up on Paul and Davey's side of the bay.

"Do you see that?" I stared at the sizzling flare while smacking Tony in the chest. My voice rose, "You see that?"

We both watched it burn, sizzling through the night sky. I noted that it didn't go over the silhouette of the mountain top, 5500 feet, before it lost its boost and descended. My spotlight was out and it was too dark to see if Paul and Davey were in trouble so we rushed to get our line off deck, hurrying to reach them before they sank.

Our 8-71 Jimmy engine only pushes our boat 14 knots when the turbo is running and we rarely went full throttle because it sucked double the fuel. But that night I powered away to get to the other side.

When I motored up to them they were casually dropping their line, looking like nothing was amiss.

I called out, "Did you shoot off that flare?"

Davey gave me a perplexed look. "Huh?"

"Did you shoot off a flare?" I glanced past their deck

light, toward their wheel house to see if I could see their flare gun.

"No," Paul replied.

I thought he was joking.

Beside me, Tony called out, "Are you sure you didn't shoot up a flare?"

"Hey, we're changing a line." Davey looked like he'd worked the midnight shift. "Why would we shoot a flare?"

"Did you see any other boat come into the bay?"

Paul looked at Davey before answering, "I haven't seen another boat since we left port."

"Where was the flare?"

"Right above you."

As soon as they finished their line, we hooked The Little Mule to The Four Seasons and headed for Kemano, an Alcan Aluminum electrical plant, to report the flare. Since Paul and Davey hadn't shot off the flare, we assumed the flare had to come from another boat that had slipped into the bay without us noticing.

Not quite an hour later we tied up to their dock.

Kemano is a unique electrical plant that was built into a mountain. Out in the middle of nowhere, it can only be accessed by boat or plane in winter. Its eight generators sit 1400 feet inside the base of Mt Dubose in a cavern that was blasted out of solid rock. Built in the 1950's, it generates 896 MW of power. It was the largest and costliest power plant by a private company in B.C., during its time. The town housed approximately 220 personnel.

A year prior, I had done some construction there and was fortunate to have taken a tour inside the mountain that housed the generators. The complex was impressive. I recall walking down a long tunnel, when we came to the area the generators were planted, the rock ceiling opened up so high and wide that it made me pause – quite remarkable.

At Kemano's dock, I used their radio to talk to security. They were 10 miles down the road, in their little town. I reported the flare, figuring it came from one of their boats, perhaps from their yacht club.

Their radio man replied, "Except for the Nechako, our ferry vessel, there have been no other boats out of Kemano in the last few months."

Walking back to our boat, I was perplexed – who shot off the flare? The next closest town was Kitimat, where we all lived, some 65 miles away. Except for a small logging operation, and Kemano, it was uninhabited country and I mean uninhabited.

The wind had picked up and, with The Little Mule in tow, and another dock in front of us, the guys were unable to push The Four Seasons off the dock without the wind blowing it back. The Four Seasons is substantially larger than The Little Mule and the wind was keeping both in check so I told Paul to take The Little Mule into the harbor so I could back The Four Season's out. An argument ensued because he wanted us to do it with ropes, but I could see the wind was too strong. It wasn't a shouting affair but nerves were touchy at times when we'd all been cooped up together for so long.

There was a good chop in the harbor and I guess Paul didn't want to buck the waves in The Little Mule while waiting. I can't blame him, but with that boat in tow and a dock perpendicular to us, there was no other way.

I found when working with guys in tight quarters it wasn't the big stuff that put us at odds, but the small stuff. Guys not cleaning up behind themselves when they use the toilet, or picking their nose too much when they prepare food or hanging their damp shirts too close to the stove, those kinds of things really spark the grumbles.

We used our radar when we motored at night. As we traveled we talked about the odds of the flare coming from the plane the previous night. That long shot was looking like a possibility.

But it was such a remote possibly that Paul asked me, "Did you really see a flare?"

I thumbed toward Tony. "He saw it too."

Cruising back into Chief Mathews Bay, I swept along the shoreline we'd seen the flare and honked our air horn a few times, telling whoever might be up there that we knew he was alive. We anchored and began boxing prawns.

About an hour later the Nechako ferry arrived. This was Alcan's ferry that worked between Kitimat and Kemano.

Obviously my message had gone down the line. It was good to see them show support, coming with a full crew.

I talked via radios and told them where we had seen the flare. They patrolled the shoreline, flashing their spotlight up to that area and honked their horn.

Their captain reiterated, "No other boats have been out of our harbor for over a month."

Before they left they motored close enough that we didn't have to use our radios. It was always so formal and blunt to use the machines. I told them about the plane we heard the night prior, but I probably used some weak adjectives in my conclusion. The odds of a plane going down in the mountains in front of us and someone surviving seemed too surreal to be true. There was no mystery about it. I think under the surface those who hadn't seen the flare treated it like some alien spaceship story, an impossible event.

As we drifted closer, one of their crew mentioned the

logging camp that was on the other side of the mountain. "Maybe the flare came from one of their guys."

I retorted, "I don't think so because that flare fizzled out before it crested the mountains. It would take some real Superman to crest those mountains with all that snow up there."

Then there was the remote possibility that a boat had come up from Kitimat and cruised into the bay without us noticing, plowed into a rock and fired off a flare before sinking. This possibility was as remote as the plane because few boats sailed out that time of year and even fewer motored that far down Gardner Channel as there was no place to refuel. Moreover, there weren't any underwater rock formations to hit on that side of the bay; the landscape was too steep.

I don't know what the Nechako's crew did with the news of the circling jet. When you're young, and you're dealing with the unknown, I know that I wasn't that confident. Half of coping is an act and one tends to joke too much about the what-if's, and that can shift the focus. I'm glad I wasn't the only one who'd seen the flare because second guessing was thick and rightfully so. Considering how few commercial fishing boats were out that time of year, what were the odds of a plane crash landing in the same bay that we were fishing when British Columbia is nearly three times the size of California and has a vast coastline? I doubt there would be more than a handful of boats out. With that, who's to say any of their crew would be outside that time of night to even hear a plane? And with all that hellacious weather, pilots know enough to stay above the clouds. Furthermore, how many planes fall out of the sky along that entire coast in one month? I bet there's less than two. Truly, if this were a fictional story, one would have to say it was too unreal to be believed.

Nechako's crew didn't linger long before heading back to Kemano. They had access to the outside world. We hoped that they'd put two and two together with any reports of a missing plane and send a helicopter to the rescue.

By 9:00 pm we finished boxing prawns. It was another quiet dinner as we devoured every morsel. Dead tired after working since early morning, it was always good to eat warm food then crawl into bed. That Isuzu diesel that ran the freezer was a lot more rackety than the 8-71 turbo that ran the main screw, but it was never bothersome enough to prevent sleep from pulling me under.

Our day started around 6am. I headed down in the engine room to check the oil and Freon levels. This was one of the few times I turned off the engines. Though there wasn't much room to move around, it was always nice and warm; I liked the look of the engine's alpine green paint. I have good memories of that engine room and hearing the sea lap upon the fiberglass. With the engine shut off, it was quiet enough to say my morning prayers.

From there, I joined the guys who were on shifts in the freezer room. We took turns because it was difficult to spend more than 15 minutes at -30 F. Our rubber raingear got stiff in those conditions.

I always liked to see my breath crystallize when I climbed down that ladder. Once there, it was a race to get the boxes moved off the freezer plates, opened, laid out on the floor, and then sprayed with water a number of coats, hopefully before our fingers and feet froze. Good gloves and boots helped but moving quickly was the key. We'd stop spraying the prawns when they got about a ¼ inch of ice covering. They were to be eaten in Sushi bars so the quality had to be there.

Being down in that icy hold was like a slap in the face that forced you to dance. If you were lethargic, it was a great way to start a day. On exiting, it was always refreshing to come up the ladder into warmer conditions. Freezer work would made a cold, dreary, 25 F morning seem rather balmy.

Our days were a race from morning to night; a workaholic's dream. The only time we weren't on the go was when we were traveling from one bay to the next. We had eight miles of line that we picked up and dropped off daily. When a line came in, we snapped traps off, averaging one every 13 seconds. During that time, I had to engage and disengage the drum via a hydraulic switch, occasionally steer the boat with another hydraulic switch, work the throttle, snap the trap off the line, open the trap and shake the prawns out, rip the old bait clear then flip it over for the next guy.

Tony would reload the trap with new bait before stacking it.

Sometimes the long line snaps (a stainless spring loaded clamp) weren't the easiest to disengage, but I never felt stronger. Doing that near 400 times a day in choppy weather will turn your core into a rock. At times in this ever-straining work, my stomach muscles would cramp up. Whoever thought stomach muscles would cramp up? Though painful, it was almost comical.

When we got underway, I thought I saw movement by the shore. On closer observation, I saw it was a mountain goat. With the snow behind him his white hair made him difficult to see but his black horns stood out. There were four goats meandering down to the salt.

It was one of those rare sunny mornings that are so glorious when they appear. Snow's brilliant crispness came right down to the water's edge and hung in the tips of the evergreens. We had just picked up the line that Paul and Davey had dropped off the night before. I was going through the motions, hooking the rope up to the drum when I heard what sounded like an aluminum door banging shut. This noise was clearly from up the slope where we'd seen the flare.

Looking at Tony, I asked, "What did that sound like to you?"

"It sounded like an aluminum door shutting." Tony somberly looked up the mountain side.

"That's exactly what it sounded like to me."

I tossed our line and buoy overboard and radioed Paul, telling him to get rid of their line because they were going to be trekking up the mountain.

As I previously mentioned, all of that topography was steep country, rising quickly out of the bay. I wanted to go with them but with the twenty foot tides, and no dingy to leave on shore, someone had to stay with the boats. Watching the guys disappear into the trees, I envied their hike.

While Tony, Paul and Davey searched for the plane, I spent the time doing paper work and cleaning up. We had to submit our catch numbers to BC Fisheries, and I wanted to make sure mine were in order.

As with any fishery, our survival depended on profit. Part of the problem with prawn fishing was there was so little money in it; the product had to be perfectly frozen, the prawns glazed a number of times to keep the quality the Sushi bars wanted as they were eaten raw. Everything had to be just so, or you wouldn't receive the high price, and the high price was barely enough for us to survive. Additionally, the buyer was like a raven, searching for anything to peck you down. There was no room for error.

Our plight was always staying ahead of the bill collector. If those engines were running then we had to be moving, placing product on those freezer plates because, in that country, fuel and food weren't cheap. Nothing was cheap in coastal B.C.. Since purchasing that freezer boat, a year prior, the wife and I had only made ends meet by extending bank loans. I didn't want to admit it but knew if the present trip didn't pan out the game would go into the fourth quarter. The stress of this caused the back of my knees to break out with this yellowy gooey substance.

Interestingly, my brother, who owned a few nurseries, had the same problem when winter would hit and income was low.

During that time in my life, being a tithe paying Christian, I believed that God was somehow going to make it happen, somehow going to provide for my family. Though, when the bank account was emptying out, it was starting to get more and more trying.

In looking back, when I consider the trials and stress of a small business person in this country who has to deal with the onslaught of bills, payroll taxes and now health insurance, then hear about some new tax the government monkeys are planning, I want to shout, "What are you thinking!"

There's a time coming, if not at hand, when those who were considering striking out on their own, will say, "It's not worth it" and stay with their lifeless job in the dreary corporate world. It is unfortunate because enterprisers are the heroes of the economy, the drivers of nearly all job creation in most countries.

Paul, Davey and Tony spent a good five hours up the mountain, searching for that pilot.

When they returned, I motored over to pick them up. As I neared shore, it was spooky to hear my talking sounder say, "Ten, zero seven, zero five, zero three . . . ohh, ohh." I put it in reverse and warily looked out the portside window to see how deep it was.

The bow crept toward Paul who was on the water's edge, waiting. The Four Season's nose met him near eye level. Grabbing the rail, he muscled up. With help from others, he swung up, boarding. Davey and Tony followed.

While backing away from shore, I impatiently waited to hear their story.

Paul stepped down the wheelhouse stairs. "There's so much snow up there that plane could be twenty feet away and you wouldn't see it."

"How far you get?"

"I got to a certain point where there was a bit of a valley, but it's slight. It's so steep; everything on both sides is billygoat country."

Davey said the same thing, "We're pushing through over three feet of snow, maybe four." He shook his head. "If the pilot's truly there, you could walk right by him and not see him."

Tony added, "There's too much snow. You could spend a month up there looking for him and not find him."

"Did you guys call out to him?"

"Yeah, sometimes I yelled."

"I heard Tony yapp'en."

I knew then that rescuing that pilot was bigger than us. I had to get others involved.

With The Little Mule in tow, I powered The Four Seasons toward Kemano again.

When we came into their harbor, I was surprised to see a 500 foot vessel parked at the dock. It was a Canadian government vessel, having traveled up the coast to change out the batteries in the buoys.

In my worn green raingear, I went up their gangway to talk with the captain. When I entered that ship, I don't doubt I smelled like a dead fish. Seeing how well groomed all the deckhands were, I felt kind of grubby.

A man in a Canadian Coast Guard navy blue suit guided me to the captain's office. This office was to be envied, over 400 square feet with a large wooden desk, and his first mate was a brunette beauty.

The captain was an older, short man who was glancing at his watch before I began my plane story.

This time, I was very clear about the plane, hitting on all three points, hearing the jet engine several times on that stormy snowy night, seeing the flare and hearing the aluminum door shut.

I was hardly finished when he said, "A red flare's not marine. It's none of our business."

It was right around whiskey time for him; I could see his collection off to the side. I supposed this unshaven fisherman's welcome was spent. I glanced at his beauty while trying to keep in check some rising frustrations, suggesting, "You can call Victoria and check their records for a downed plane. It happened just the other night."

The words were hardly out of my mouth when he countered, "The press will get a hold of it and blow it up."

I was taken aback by his negativity, his lack of compassion. Glaring at him, I forced down a growl. "You have to do something."

"But you never saw this plane?"

"Right, but I heard an aluminum door shut."

"And who's to say that wasn't from your other boat? Sound does have a tendency to travel over water." He looked out his window. "I see there's an aluminum door on your skiff."

"I can assure you that sound came from up the mountain." I found softer tones, pleading, "What does it matter if it were a red flare or white flare, the guy's got red blood in his veins?"

Gathering his thoughts, he looked cold and distant, glancing about the room.

Angered, I stated, "I will tell you something: we've spent our resources, we've stopped fishing and we've gone up the mountain looking for him. This is our second trip to Kemano. I'm out of resources here." My hand rose and I wanted to point it at him, but I checked myself. "I'll tell you what, when I get back to Kitimat, I'll tell the press a story that you won't like and I know your boat name." I was shaking when I finished.

There were no cordial goodbyes. I found my way out and the long walk down their gangway felt even longer.

When I motored back to Chief Mathews Bay I thought about that government man who was more concerned with the press blowing out some story rather than making the call on behalf of a downed pilot. And here he was the captain of a Coast Guard ship. I really didn't get that.

That night, seeing the poor results from our traps, we all knew we had to be moving on. I didn't like this and wished we had more resources to keep looking for the intangible pilot, but my finances were underwater. We had our own fight for survival.

Paul concurred, "Even if he still alive, with all that snow who's to say we'd ever find him."

Tony added, "We could spend a month up there and still not find him."

Before going to bed, I tried not to think about that pilot, but I knew with the cold and possible injuries, he had to have another miracle now. I said a prayer for him.

Mid-morning, we had picked up our traps and were getting ready to head out. Paul and Davey were onboard, and The Little Mule was in tow.

"Look at that." Paul pointed toward Gardner Channel. We couldn't miss that great Coast Guard vessel, cruising around the point.

The radio ignited, "We're intending to send men ashore. Where can we park?"

The hair on my arm rose at his words. I excitedly radioed back, "You can have the entire bay, we've pulled our gear." What an exhilarating sight to see their immense ship coming to the rescue.

"Yeah, baby!" Tony pumped his fist.

Davey pointed toward the eastern sky. "Look there. You see it?"

The Cavalry, a helicopter, swept across the sky, rapidly passing the Coast Guard Vessel. It was tremendous to hear it thumping. Hope was in the air. It moved along the side of the mountain where the plane had gone down.

The Coast Guard ship motored past us, heading down the center of Chief Mathew's Bay with a crew of ninety. I could see them readying a flat bottomed boat atop that was every bit as big as The Four Seasons.

It was also exciting to hear that the captain was sending

a crew ashore, such encouraging words, so relieving to see the big boys come to town. I had a totally new attitude toward the captain, may God Bless him. I was sure they'd find the pilot now. Thank you, Jesus.

I write this account August, 2017, thirty-two years after these events. Certain memories come up, yet others are forgotten, but I know we motored back and lined them up to where we thought that plane was.

In our wheelhouse, we talked cheerfully. Maybe the plane's pilot had a broken leg and some frostbite, but he would mend. Fate was on his side.

The helicopter made a quick sweep along the mountain side, slowing in a few places then turned and headed back from where it came, cutting across the channel, sweeping toward Kemano with speed. Interestingly, he didn't seem to be there for over twenty minutes.

We were nearly out of the bay when I radioed over, "Did the helicopter find him?"

I could see the Coast Guard deck hands in the midst of craning off their landing vessel when their radio man broke the airwaves, "Negative."

Unfortunately, that was the last of my communications with them. We motored around the point and continued up Gardner Channel. It was one of our few breaks where we ate and played cards. Canasta was the favorite game.

Talk was more upbeat; the crew from the Coast Guard would surely find him. There was a bunch of them.

Around noon The Four Seasons cruised through an area in the channel where the weather abruptly changed. It was somewhere along Whidbey Reach when the coastal air met inland air, and a twenty degree drop in temperature drifted through. That should've warned me but I wasn't listening; my mind was still on the helicopter pilot. That, "negative," was bugging me. I found it perplexing. Pray tell the downed aircraft wasn't completely covered in snow.

We dropped our traps in Kitlope Anchorage.

It was dark when we tied up to a couple of logs that some logging operation had set for a dock. The shore made an abrupt ninety degree turn there, and a narrow waterfall flowed in the background, making an ideal cove. On either end, heavy cabling ran right up and around some trees. We tied The Little Mule up to the inside of the logs and The Four Seasons to the outside.

It was unnatural how cold it was getting, like a frozen blanket had descended. When we boxed the prawns that night, I had never gone back to the wheelhouse so many times to warm my fingers. Though I did enjoy that waterfall, sometimes one's alertness to weather changes can be numbed by overwork. As I walked to the wheelhouse, I do remember our overhead lights reflecting off the bay's water which was checking, freezing up.

We all admired the waterfall, so refreshing to hear it splash into that cozy corner of Kitlope Anchorage. With over 170 inches of participation, waterfalls were common in that rain forest. The channel's salt water is near 50/50 fresh which raises the freezing point.

A WAKE UP CALL

The next morning I struggled out of our sleeping quarters, half dressed and half dozy. Relief descended when I turned off the engine. Silence was friendly. I snagged my grey wool undershirt off a clothes line and pulled it over a t-shirt. The boat was so incredibly silent that it was somewhat bewildering. Stepping toward the back door, I looked out its window at the waterfall. No water appeared to be moving. On closer observation I saw it was frozen solid. I was amazed yet threatened. Viewing the bay, I saw it was covered with an eerie sheet of ice. This was no joke.

I hurried back to the sleeping quarters and called down, "Hey guys, get up. Everything's frozen out there."

It was another scramble with no rest for the wicked. When I stepped out on deck, my rubber boot slid across the ice covered fiberglass, and I nearly ate the deck. Some of these acts of nature will really keep you on your toes. If I wasn't careful, I could slide out the opening where the traps came up. Unfortunately, we didn't have any sand to spread on deck to give our boots a better grip.

Even the logs on the log boom that Paul and Davey had to step over to reach The Little Mule were icy. Overnight the ice in the bay had grown nearly an inch thick. I groaned, having $20,000.00 worth of fishing gear imprisoned under it.

Worse yet, The Little Mule was locked in place by ice. The 115 hp Suzuki engine was unable to break it free. With the big boat, I drove in circles, making waves to crack it up. At last this action freed The Little Mule. Thank God. The crunching sound the bow made when it cut through the ice was quite ominous.

The sides of The Four Seasons were less than a ½ inch thick fiberglass. I mumbled more than once, "Hold together baby."

When I let off the throttle there was little drift before the boat stopped.

I knew we had till dark to get our gear and sorry hides out of that bay. I'll never forget that day. The Northern wintery wonderland was at its best, under a striking blue sky; the cold blanketed, glistening and crisp, locking everything firmly. It was as if Old Man Winter were shouting, "I am incredible!"

Paul and Davey found some way of going through that ice to get to the other side of the bay. I don't remember seeing them again till dark. All of us had worked the summer months in fishing, but none had worked the winter months. It was quite something to see the rising line, stretched, cutting through the ice like a blade, then the trap breaking through the ice.

When water dripped off the pulley and hit the top of my raingear hood, it instantly froze. I was constantly knocking icicles off my hood's visor. Any water that dripped off the pulley and ended up with the prawns in the red totes instantly froze. I bet it was colder on deck than in our freezer.

Looking down along the side of the boat, I noticed any

water that splashed up on the gunnels froze. It was unsettling that the ice was getting thicker. Sometimes, when a trap came up, the Japanese snap wouldn't break the ice. We could see the poly line sliding through it and the trap hanging just below. When the next prawn trap hit, both traps broke through, and I'd have to stop the drum because I had two traps to deal with. This happened a number of times, which slowed us down.

This was the first time we had tanner crab as a supplementary catch. How those crabs got into our three inch openings was a mystery. Generally we tossed anything supplementary overboard. But this time when we tossed those crabs over they just sat atop the ice. The seagulls had a field day with them.

Tony took one of those tanners and gave it a heave. It slid atop the ice, spinning for over thirty yards before the seagulls pounced.

We caught an eel that was over a foot long with rows and rows of teeth and the way he swung back and forth, snapping at us, proved that he wasn't happy in our good company. I left him atop a hatch cover to let him cool down a bit. About ten minutes later I moved my finger by his face. He still tried to get it but at -30F, he was an eighth of his speed. When you deal with so much repetition, changing hundreds of traps, day after day, little beasts like that eel were entertaining.

The most challenging catch were octopus. Their mouth is like a parrot's beak but more deadly. Its beak can break right through a crab's back. They are also called devil fish as they are good killers. Once, we caught this fancy looking eel and were keeping it alive in fresh salt water in one of our red totes, hoping that it was something really rare that would free us from all the debt we were in. We also caught a little octopus that was about 5 inches long.

Curious to see what it would do with our eel, I set him in the tote's water. This tote was about two feet by a foot and a half with about 13" of water in it. It was fascinating to see how quickly that octopus figured out what it needed to do to capture that eel. It hadn't swum around that red tote two minutes before it stealthfully swam over our precious then spread its legs wide, and drifted down. Another second it would've had our beauty.

Scientists say an octopus have eyes that are very close to human's. Go figure. Anytime they entered our traps, they killed every prawn, nothing but shells left. Octopus aren't friends of fishermen.

Little by little we collected our lines, pulling them out of the ice.

Darkness fell. We hooked up The Little Mule before snagging our last line. This line was outside the bay, just past Queens Point, where there was open water, no ice from then on. The line was in a precarious spot because it was so close to shore. This wouldn't have been a big deal had we not had The Little Mule in tow and I had not missed the first buoy of the prawn line, much to do with no spotlight. I was constantly afraid of hitting the shore and chided myself for not spending the $90.00 to replace the spotlight. But what do you do when you're out of funds? Additionally, with the wind and waves, that darn Little Mule kept banging our stern. We had tires back there to prevent damage, but the impact unnerved me, and I wondered if the window in The Little Mule would pop out. The wind had picked up, and it was blowing opposite to the direction that was favorable.

This wind was relentless, pushing us in the wrong direction. I was about to tell Paul to disconnect The Little

Mule and go out in the channel and wait for us. I knew he didn't like re-boarding at night so I made an impatient circle of the boat. In doing so, I caught a trap on the propeller. Oh boy. My heart dropped when I heard the thump, thump, of the stainless ring on the keel. This was bad. If that trap or line worked its way through the rubber that encased the prop, it would be game over for us.

For a second I was breathless, unsure what to do. Then I shut down the engine and sent up a prayer. Now we had a line of thirty traps dangling from the prop, with the wind blowing, and the shore within 200 feet. The moon wasn't up yet, so it was dark.

The battle then was between the wind and the dangling prawn line that was attached like an anchor to our prop. Stepping down into the wheelhouse, I went to look in the radar to see our position. Its green line blazed around the dark screen, outlining the shore. Thankfully, the wind was strong enough to push us away from shore. Even though we had a string of traps hanging from our prop, the wind kept pushing us farther out. I imagined the line was getting stretched.

We all took turns putting our faces in the radar, checking our position. Then the line broke. There went a lot of money. We could feel The Four Seasons suddenly drift faster.

Since the wind was pushing us down the middle of the channel, I decided to have dinner before our next move. The guys were always gung-ho to have dinner. While we ate, we checked our position on the radar. It was still good. The wind was doing its best to keep us in the middle of the channel.

After dinner I started the main diesel and barely moved the throttle forward, listening to see if the trap were still there. Again that thump, thump, thump against the keel. I quickly turned the engine off.

"Paul, Davey, get a rope and The Little Mule and bring it around to the bow. You'll have to tow us."

In short order they boarded The Little Mule and after refilling its heater, they powered it around to hook up The Four Seasons.

We didn't have to box prawns that night because our catch was frozen solid in the red totes, glazed over with endless drips of water from off the pulley. We were going to have to try to sell them locally; no Sushi bar would want them.

I sat behind the wheel while The Little Mule towed us down the channel. Time passed before a half moon appeared. It gave good light, reflecting off the snow covered mountains. Nodding over the wheel, I tried to fight off sleep. Tony was washing dishes.

I thought about our next move. It might be best to dock at Kemano and the following morning do the jump-over-board thing to see if I could free that trap from the propeller. I wasn't looking forward to it because the propeller was six feet under, and I didn't have a wetsuit. It was nuts how cold that water was.

I had fallen asleep when we came up on the outskirts of Chief Mathews Bay. When I awoke, I saw The Little Mule was stopped, up on ice. Paul and Davey had hustled out of the wheelhouse, their arms waving. The Four Season's bow was heading straight at them, about to crush their Suzuki outboard.

My drowsiness instantly disappeared – I fired up the diesel, threw it in reverse, and rammed the throttle down.

Paul told me later the front edge of the bow just touched the top of that outboard motor before backing away.

The trap that was on the prop of The Four Seasons was thrown off. There was no more, thump, thump when I put it in gear. Why didn't I think to reverse the prop earlier?

We were all stunned to see a sheet of ice coming out of Chief Mathews Bay, going straight across Gardner Channel, clear to the other side. It was two inches thick. How bizarre to think that we had pulled out of that bay not even two days prior!

I pulled The Four Seasons in front of The Little Mule and hooked it up. After Paul and Davey climbed aboard, we started plowing through that ice. This time, when I let off the throttle, the boat instantly stopped – no drift whatsoever. Midway through this area, I was getting concerned because the sound of it cutting along the fiberglass hull was fearsome.

Sometimes at that age, the pride and power of life would overwhelm me and I acted as if I weren't afraid of anything, with a kind of cavalier attitude, but not that night. When cutting through the ice, my wary eyes went to shore as I calculated the distance back to Kemano. If the ice punched through our hull, we'd have to swim to shore before we tramped ten miles along the steep shoreline, through the snow to get to their dock. My wife, Elaine, and kids seemed very far away then.

It was such a starry, moon filled night that we all ended up on the bridge above the wheelhouse, taking it all in.

Paul asked me to stop. I pulled the throttle back. The boat abruptly stopped, with The Little Mule bumping into our stern. Paul descended the ladder to the main deck, took hold of the railing, using the icy gunnels as a step, before slowly lowering himself. He stepped onto the ice. Below him was the ice covered channel.

"Don't let go of that railing," I warned.

He disregarded my warning and released his grip. "Look Mom, no hands."

I was relieved the ice didn't crack.

Paul climbed back and we motored on.

I'll never forget that night. The magical beauty of the moonlight reflecting off the snow-covered mountains and the ice filled bay were magnificent sights to see. It was as if God were performing a symphony. Though it was cold out, we were all in awe at the beauty around us. Still, with the continual crushing sound of that ice cutting along our fiberglass hull, I was starting to wonder if it would ever end.

Paul gazed at me in wonderment. "It's as if God is taking us through the eye of the needle."

"No doubt."

At last we broke into open waters. FREE! The Four Seasons came through like a champ though we wore more than 1/8 inch off the pointed fiberglass bow. I noticed right away how much faster she sped. On closer inspection, I found the inch thick slime that grew on the bottom was gone. It was clean white, like a new hull and we went nearly two knots faster than normal using the same rpm.

Glancing back at the ice that spanned the channel and Chief Mathews Bay, I knew if there were a downed pilot out there that he'd certainly die of exposure. There was no doubt; it was too cold for anyone to make it without heat.

When we passed the lights of Kemano's harbor, I was thankful I didn't have to dive into that bay and swim under the boat to free that prawn trap from the propeller. Thank God.

Using our radar, we continued down the dark channel for Kitimat. Heading for home was always fun.

Ironically, Kitimat, means – valley of the snow – in the

Haisla language. The Haisla tribe has a village at the end of Douglas Channel while the town of Kitimat is only fifteen minutes from the docks. Kitimat is on the map because of Alcan Aluminum, and Alcan's smelter is on the map because of Kemano. I suppose you need a certain amount of electrical power to convert bauxite into aluminum.

On the boat we had a saying, "If you've been to Kitimat, Terrace and Prince Rupert then you've been around the world." In reality, we should've included Kemano.

CASUALTIES

The next day, we offloaded our prawns at the government dock at the end of Kitimat Village. This was our first substantial load. I figured over $10,000.00 at the wholesalers. As I say, there wasn't much money in it. It's a mystery how it can get in your blood though.

I was excited to see Elaine and the kids. Paul's wife and kids came down to the dock, too.

The prawn wholesaler was in Vancouver, 900 miles south. I hired a trucking company to freight it. In hindsight I should've bought insurance on the load but we were too stretched financially to pay an extra $600.00.

As it turned out, the truck was misrouted, ended up in Blaine, Washington, and sat in a yard for a few days. I'm not so sure if their freezers went out somewhere, but was told by the wholesaler in Vancouver that our prawns lost their glaze and had to be sold for seconds and thirds. It was terribly disappointing. The check we received hardly covered our cost for fuel and food.

I held hope that one last trip would somehow pull us out of our financial slide. April rains were beckoning. Amazingly the guys went along. There were around 600 gallons of diesel in the tank, why waste it?

Our first stop was Gardner Channel to see if we could

snag the line we lost. If we were lucky, we'd find the other buoy. We dragged for that line a full day but no luck. We went on, leaving Gardner behind, motoring to a channel we'd never fished.

We ended up in Butedale. There was a lone care taker there who was friendly enough. He told us about its history. Supposedly Butedale, in its time, was a bigger concern than San Francisco. I had a hard time believing that. Now it was nothing but a relic, dark and gloomy, ghoulish, its wood all rotten, its wharves melting into the sea. What change a 150 years will make. That place was haunting.

The fishing in that area was no good. It was as if we were on the trail of another prawn boat. Generally we fished around sixty fathoms, 360 feet. We tried different depths but to no avail.

I clearly remembered the last few days I fished. Paul had dropped off a line in quite a steep area, which is a no, no. Both buoys had disappeared. It was a long line with a lot of gear. To say I wasn't happy with his decision was an understatement. We had charts, and sometimes I wondered if he ever used them. I wasn't in the best of moods when we started dragging for the line. It is terribly boring to drop a line with an anchor-looking spiky thing, with lots of J hooks attached then drag it perpendicular to the line in hopes of catching it. It was always disheartening to power up the line to see nothing on those hooks. We did that all day long.

Coupled with no traps recovered was the rain which wouldn't stop. Each time that line came up empty, it was as if a devil were perched on my shoulder, whispering in my ear, "You failed again."

Failure wasn't new to me. I'm almost embarrassed to mention the things I tried before jumping into commercial fishing. I had started an automotive part's shop, Bumper to Bumper, then sold that because I didn't like being cooped up in one spot. Next, I partnered up with a fellow in construction and did commercial contracting, working on Alcan and Eurocan. But my mainstay was tile contracting. I had contracted jobs throughout the province, doing jobs all over the lower mainland, from Prince Rupert to Queen Charlotte Islands, right down to Mica Creek. I enjoyed seeing new places, meeting new people. However, when construction took a nose dive and I lost money on some of these adventures, then the devil was there to remind me.

The area we were fishing had a narrow entrance point with a rock wall that powered straight out of the water, very much like Half Dome in Yosemite though not nearly as tall. I felt so small when I cruised by that big rock.

Two days of that trip were wasted on dragging for lines.

Spring rains blanketed the coast. If it weren't raining, then it was clouding up to rain. That area received over ten times the rain that I was used to in California. I remember a stretch where I didn't see the sunshine for three months, nothing but dreary rain, on and on. Under the rain forest, there's a heaviness that will get to you. Being from the Sunshine State, I knew the sunshine was up there, somewhere. But with low lying clouds and rain constantly hitting my raingear, the dreariness would eventually drag on me. Those coastal areas have a high rate of suicide.

After losing that line I could see the writing on the wall with commercial fishing. The Four Seasons had to be sold. Heading for home, we motored by Butedale, the old relic of a port which was once bustling, yet now melted into the sea. I was incredibly saddened by the fact that commercial fishing for me was done. There was no mystery; I had failed.

It didn't matter how much work we put in, that horse didn't run.

The Devil's whisperings were present, "You are a failure."

At the table behind me, the guys were playing cards. It was about an hour before dusk. I was on my feet, leaning against the beam that supported the electronics, gazing out the forward windows, my focus on the dark clouds just beyond that gloomy port.

The Devil piled on, "You can't even provide for your family. . . What good are you?"

My head hurt. What good was I?

He whispered, "You're good for nothing."

Disheartened, my eyes started to water.

The devil was relentless. "You've got nowhere to go now."

The constant rain drummed over the windshield, singing with the demons. "Failure, failure, failure. And how many businesses have you tried?"

The sky grew darker, making my failures heavier. I pressed my hand into my eyes to stop a flood, forcing my head up so the guys wouldn't see.

The devil prodded, "There's more value for you in your life insurance policy than in fishing. At least you can provide for your family with the insurance. Put some weights in your boots before you step off deck, with the autopilot on, the guys won't even notice."

I gazed out the window, desperately hoping for something better, anything.

The devil wouldn't give it up, "Drowning is not bad; you can walk out of the wheelhouse and step off the deck. Now's a good time."

Abruptly, a shaft of light burst through those dark

clouds, right through the thickest clouds. It blazed down, hitting the inlet in front of the boat. Greater flashes fought the darkness back, and the entire strength of the sun was right behind, beaming straight at me.

I heard a voice, not audible but very clear, "Your future is that bright!"

It was so bright I couldn't even look at it. What a breath of fresh air. That was my Jesus! That's my God! He gives you hope when there's none. I grabbed onto it like a sinking sailor.

A DIFFERENT WORLD

At that time, since I had no tile contracts, my next option was to go down to the San Francisco Bay Area and see if I could get a job with one of the tile companies.

My brother and his wife lived in Danville, and my sister and her husband lived in Concord. They were gracious enough to put me up, staying one week with one and the next week with the other. I found work in San Francisco and sent paycheck after paycheck to Elaine in Kitimat. In the meantime, she put the boats and house up for sale.

She was pregnant with our third child. When Whitney was born, we didn't have enough money for me to go meet her. Three months later, Elaine came for a visit. I treasured seeing her and finally meeting my new daughter.

During that year by myself, before The Four Seasons was sold, I'd often dream about a way to gain enough money to buy another fishing license, maybe salmon; surely that would pay the bills. It's funny how commercial fishing gets into your blood. It was so easy to fantasize about getting back out there.

Though the struggles were great, the memories were unbeatable. One night onboard The Four Seasons, during a wintery storm, I saw movement by our large drum that wheeled in the rope. Just below the line, I noticed a blackish bird. I don't ever recall seeing a bird on deck. It looked as if it were examining some chum. How it got onboard on that stormy, windy night was a mystery. I shuffled around some gear to get closer and was surprised it didn't take off. The light was dim. As I drew closer, it looked up at me and didn't appear to be threatened in the least. I knelt, my raingear touching the deck and slowly moved my open palm toward it. It still showed no sign of fear. My palm ended right in front of its webbed feet. Inexplicably, it walked right onto my palm. I felt like a king, holding something from the heavens. Rising, I headed straight to the back of the boat where the guys were boxing prawns.

Nearing them, I stepped to my post, as if I were going to start stacking prawns into the boxes. Then I brought my arm out from behind me, slowly sweeping the bird past each one of them. This action could've stopped a Killer Whale's chase of a seal. All of them were awe struck by that bird.

I headed for the wheelhouse with the guys in tow.

We were the killers of the sea, but there was no way we'd lay a hand on this tender bird.

Just inside the wheelhouse, Davey commented, "It'd be no good if that bird died on this boat."

"It'd be bad ju-ju," Tony agreed.

I didn't put a lot of credence in that good luck/bad luck thing, but the rest of them did. You could feel their unease.

The wheelhouse door shut behind Paul.

We all moved as if the bird's life depended on it.

"It's got to be hungry." Paul hastily looked about for food.

I could see its wings were wet and started to put it on the counter next to the diesel stove to dry it out when Tony said, "I don't think that's a good idea. It's too close to the heat."

"You're right. What am I thinking? You're right."

Davey snatched a small box, cut it in half, and set it on the counter below the forward windows. "Set it here."

I had hardly set the bird into the box when it did its business.

"I hope it's not sick."

"It's got to be hungry."

"What do you think it eats?"

"Fish." Tony went to get a can of tuna fish.

I snagged a small custard cup and poured some water into it then shuffled about the guys to set it in the little box. Paul cracked some soda crackers and set them in the box.

This bird had an ebony roundish beak with a teardrop welded right in the middle of it. I chuckled to see little Teardrop walk about. Its little webbed feet were a sight. It appeared to be showing them off as it strutted about the box. Then it cocked its head back and looked each of us over.

"Here you go." Tony set a thumb full of tuna fish in the box.

Teardrop studied it then gazed up at Tony.

"It'd be no good if that bird died on this boat," Davey apprehensively warned, "That'd be no good at all."

"Don't talk about it, just don't talk about it."

"I wonder if it's getting too hot," added Davey, rather speedily, undoing his raingear. "We shouldn't let it get too hot."

"Maybe it shouldn't even be in here." Generally Tony was rather jovial but not with that bird. "We should get it out of here."

"You're right, if it got too warm it might die." With it so

wet outside, I was perplexed as to where we should put it. "But I can't see that bird not getting soaked out there."

Paul advised, "Let's put it up on the bridge, right under the steering column, you know the area where we store the ropes?"

I lifted the box and Tony and Davey took a last look.

It was still raining when I went out on deck. I did my best to lean over the box, trying to protect little Teardrop as I went up the ladder. Paul followed. We ended up on the upper deck. The spot he mentioned made sense because it was protected from the elements, yet open. I set the box down. Then I tore the front of it flat, allowing room for Teardrop to fly away.

The following morning, I was hardly dressed when I raced out on deck and climbed the ladder to see how our little stowaway was doing. I bent to look under the upper steering column. A pile of rope came into focus then an empty box. Teardrop was gone. I was happy to pick up that box. I looked toward the morning sky with a grin. That little creature sure brought us some joy on a stormy night.

When we got back to Kitimat I went to the library to see what kind of bird it was. The marking that stood out was the ebony teardrop in the middle of its nose. I found a picture that was true to its features right down to its webbed feet. It was called a Storm Petrol, and discovered one of its characteristics, *a friend of sailors*, and shows up on boats during storms. Amazing to think of the creative hand of our Heavenly Father, how He provides a little creature like that which appears in a storm – a friend of sailors.

A DIFFERENT DIRECTION

F inancially, I'd lost quite a bit in commercial fishing, but if God was handing out paychecks, I was handsomely rewarded with incredible experiences. I wouldn't trade a boatload of money for my experiences. That Northern world was fantastic. I felt very blessed, fortunate to be part of it. From its mountains, rivers, inlets, whales, porpoises, northern lights to its billygoats, grizzly, caribou, wolf, coyote, deer, moose, fox, salmon, prawns, crab, whiskey jacks, to the Canadians and their lovely women, what a great nation. And to work with those Canadians, that was big fun. As far as financial loses, I was still young and could start anew.

Eventually, I obtained my California tile contractor's license and began contracting. We did mostly commercial work, and I really enjoyed working with Mexicans. In due course, I started writing, working on a screenplay. In looking back, I wonder if the desire to write was due to the plane crash. Were the seeds of that mystery something that simply had to rise?

I wrote and wrote and did a lot of dreaming of what life would be if I could actually make it as an author.

DREAMS

There are a number of accounts in the Bible where people received a message through dreams. Joseph was told in a dream, not to be afraid to take Mary as his wife. He was also told in a dream to go to Egypt. Then in another dream he was directed to go back to Israel, before, finally, in yet another dream, to go to Galilee.

The first dream I remember turning into a future event, happened when I went to UOP Stockton. I dreamt of a brown Cadillac, with personalized license plates in a night scene. Back then I was new to dreams and didn't have a journal so I didn't write down the name on the license plate. It could've been – Spooky. If so, God has a sense of humor.

This dream played out a few months later when I got a job at a gas station on the other side of the tracks. I was working in the evening and a brown Cadillac pulled in. Soul music was rolling when a well dressed brown man popped out. He must've been quite the ladies' man as there were a few ladies in the back, and the smell of cologne was in the air. When he stepped out, he did a bit of a jig, grooving to his music, before adjusting his collar on his cape.

Thumbing toward the back, he instructed me, "Fill it up with ethyl."

I grinned at him – he was hard not to grin at. Taking the hose I searched both sides of his car for the gas cap but didn't see any. Then I looked to see if it was under the license plate. The plate was personalized – Spooky – and the dream was realized. It was so surreal that I did a second look, viewing the brown Cadillac, its long fins, before admiring its owner. He was right out of the Cracker Jack box, just grooving, dancing to this Motown song.

As I put this to pen, I know what the religious are going to say, "That dream wasn't from God but the devil. God's not going to give you a dream about some pimp pulling into the gas station with a Spooky license plate and some honeys in the back."

My question for them, "Didn't Christ die for the hookers, pimps and the rest of us sinners?"

My second dream concerned work as well. In the dream I saw the loading docks of a warehouse. To the side of the dock were steps down to where the trailers would back up. This area was vacant, empty of any delivery vehicles. Except for the concrete landing and steps, color-wise it had bland, off-white, somewhat yellowish walls. This dream came shortly after I'd entered Canada and was staying and working with my dad in tile work.

When that work ran out, I got a job downtown Vancouver at Van Horn Electric. During lunch break, my coworkers and I often played soccer at the back of the warehouse. I never noticed the dream's location then because there were bodies moving, chasing a ball, and commercial trucks were parked in that area. But one day after work I came out the back doors and descended the steps next to the loading dock. The place was vacant. I happened to glance back at the warehouse. That was when the déjàvu of the dream hit. Everything about that area was exactly as that dream foretold, including the short steps and the bland walls.

The next dream I had which came to pass was of a

commercial kitchen. I saw a quarry tile floor with the legs of a stainless steel counter. When I awoke from the dream I wondered if I were heading back into commercial kitchen work like I'd done in Lake Tahoe as a teen during the summers. I was somewhat disappointed because I didn't figure cooking paid enough to provide for a family; at the time I was hoping to marry Elaine.

It wasn't but a few months after the dream that I had a job with a tile company on The Four Seasons Hotel, downtown Vancouver, and we were tiling their main kitchen area. Though the kitchen was quite large, there wasn't room for a mortar mixer outside so we were mixing the mortar bed with shovels and hoes inside. It was a mindless task of pure grunt work.

A number of months after we'd completed the installation on that kitchen floor, I had gone back to do a patch job on the grout under some dishwasher machines. When I left, I turned out the light and reached for the door to exit. The door had a small glass window, allowing the light from the other room to shine in on the tile floor. Right there I saw the dream realized down to the exact way the shadows portrayed the stainless steel counter.

Interestingly, my interpretation of that dream was different than the way it played out. First I thought I'd be going back to cooking in a commercial kitchen; instead I ended up tiling one. Regardless, I can only attribute those dreams to God, assuring me that He was taking care of me.

One dream I had actually saved my life. This occurred on The Four Seasons. At night, my biggest fear was the anchor line not holding. With winter winds a howling, I imagined the anchor slipping or the line breaking. Within minutes, we'd be up on shore. One would need a number of miracles to survive on shore on those wet, cold, remote islands. This worry haunted me on windy nights when I lay in bed and heard waves splashing over the fiberglass.

This recurring nightmare was so real I'd sit up quickly and smack my forehead on the plywood bunk above. After pressing my hand into my sore head, my next move was to roll out of bed.

Shortly after, I'd be in the wheelhouse, turning on the radar machine. Antsy, I would stare out the dark windows, impatiently waiting for it to warm up. At last, I'd put my face into the rubber grommet to check our location. It was always the same spot where we anchored, thank God.

But one night we were in a bay, where, from the shape of it and the height of the mountains, I would've thought we were better protected from the winds. Not so. It was if they tore straight across the Pacific to barrel down on us. All night the boat jerked, pulling against the anchor line. The same worrisome nightmare played out and, again, I smacked my head on the plywood bunk above. After rolling out of bed, I leaned against it to get my bearings. I smelled something unfamiliar . . . smoke?

Opening the forward door, I was met by flames. Paul's shirt had fallen off the clothes hanger onto the diesel stove, caught fire and rolled onto the floor. It lay on the plywood flooring which was diesel soaked. Flames leapt toward other hanging shirts. I scrambled across the floor, grabbed the unburned end of the shirt's fabric and couldn't throw it outside the wheelhouse fast enough. Had the fire developed it would've been a disaster.

Having told Paul a number of times not to get his shirt too close to the stove, anger rose in me. It wasn't dispelled before I got everyone up and did some barking. Regardless, this dream, this nightmare of the anchor line not holding, actually saved our lives.

Years later, on a little vacation in the Nevada desert, February, 1990, I had a dream on a cold night. I had pitched my tent not far from a big hydro line. That night I had a bizarre dream of Mike Tyson losing a boxing match. At the time, Ironman Tyson was undefeated, undisputed, 37-0, heavyweight champion of the world. He'd won his previous fight in an early knockout and his boxing greatness was so well known that he was like King Kong. So much so, I recall waking up from the dream with a smirky grin because I thought that was the stupidest dream ever. Mike Tyson was The Man, and he wasn't ever going to lose.

Little did I know of a forthcoming fight between Tyson and Buster Douglas a week later on February 11 in Japan. The odd makers had Douglas a 42-1 underdog. Additionally, Douglas had lost his mom earlier in the month and he'd caught the flu a day prior the fight.

You can guess what happened. Douglas knocked Tyson out. I heard about it the following day. Even though I had the dream, I was just as surprised as everyone else. The upset was considered one of the biggest upsets in sport's history.

There must be something about the Nevada desert because I had another dream there. It concerned fiber optics. I clearly saw all these clear cables within a cable and was given the understanding that it was going to be the next big thing. How I wish I would've invested in fiber optics then because it certainly has been a hum dinger in the communication world.

I've had a number of foretelling dreams since then but most of them I didn't write down. Elaine finally told me that I should get a dream journal. In the last 8 years over half my dreams have been of a night scene with no lights.

I found them curious because they were in a powerless world. It made no sense to walk through a dark shopping mall. It made no sense to be looking at a house for sale in a dark world where the only light came from candles.

Sometime before 4:00 am on Feb 3, 2008, I had a dream that involved the world economy. I thought this was relevant because there had been some trembling in the Japanese bond market. However, I can't say I knew when this dream would play out.

In this dream, I was aboard an extremely large derelict ship. It appeared abandoned. From the upper decks, I looked toward the bow. There were several decks on the ship that cascaded down and much of their draining system was blocked by the debris of dead crabs and sea weed. This ship was shaped like a destroyer, its color dark as iron, but it had no guns. Its decks looked like they could've been used for a passenger ship, though it was difficult to imagine that, because it wasn't pretty. Everything was hard and abandoned.

The ship sat in a dead calm bay in a remote area along the British Colombia coast. I saw no other boats or signs of civilization.

The air was cool so it was either fall or spring, more likely fall because there was no snow in the mountains.

I was startled when, behind me, someone put a hand on my shoulder. It was the captain.

He said, "We have to meet up with another ship along the east coast of South America but we're too big to go through the Panama Canal and we don't have enough fuel to go around the Cape."

His words weren't out of his mouth before the ship flipped, rolling completely over.

I found myself swimming for my life, trying to reach

the boat's keel. The captain swam up behind, helping me, and we struggled up the steep hull, monkeying up the keel. At last I looked over the ship's upside down hull – it was massive, going on and on.

Soaking wet, I asked the captain, "What is this?"

"The world's economy."

I'm not sure what the full interpretation of this dream is. I once thought it had something to do with the summer Olympics in Brazil, but that date came and went. Perhaps it has something to do with a South American government going bankrupt. Maybe that will be the catalyst that starts the chain of events that eventually rolls the world's economic ship. Then again, because the captain wanted to meet up with another ship but couldn't, might have something to do with trade or the lack thereof. A trade war? I don't know. And I don't know when it will occur, but the dream was clear: the economy went belly up.

THE PLANE CRASH

Mark Twain said, "A lie can travel halfway around the world while truth is putting on its shoes." Thank God truth gets out of bed. My first book in a fictional series I wrote, called *Everyone Left Behind, 4 Minutes to Chaos*, took a little over five years to write. Those years were probably the most challenging in my life. Our finances were tapped, and Elaine came down with cancer. We couldn't afford medical insurance, so it was difficult. But through these hardships I have clearly seen the hand of my Maker. He was faithful to heal Elaine.

My second book, *Everyone Left Behind, The Roan*, took about a year and a half to complete.

I had been working on the third book in the series when an interesting turn of events took place, interrupting everything; the Canadian plane crash resurfaced.

Years earlier, I had tracked down the phone number of the helicopter pilot who had swept across that snow-covered mountainside when the Canadian Coast Guard vessel arrived.

He said they never found the plane.

"Did you fly through there in the summertime?"

"Yes."

"Any sign of it?"

"None."

These calls were spread out over the years. The third time I called he was resistant when I told him that I was going to head out there and see if I could find it.

"You can't go into that country," he firmly declared, "that's Indian country."

His resistance was perplexing. Was it truly Indian country or did he know something about that plane that he didn't want me to know?

Interestingly, I had contacted a native from Kitimat Village who gave me a quote for chartering his boat out there, and he wasn't resistant about my going there.

The resistance of that helicopter pilot piqued my interest, so I began searching for that plane in using Google Earth. However, their satellite view wasn't giving up its secret easily. Google Earth didn't allow me to zoom in enough and they don't update their imagining that often in remote areas. They allow you to zoom in on cities, not so out in the sticks.

Another problem was that mountainous terrain received so much snow that it did not quite melt off in summer before it snowed again. So finding a plane via satellite imagery was difficult. I searched every area where I thought the plane might have gone down, though I knew it was a waste of time if it were under a glacier.

Then one August day, 2017, I found new satellite imagery. Right off, something caught my eye. I zoomed in on an object that didn't look like it was made by nature. Zooming closer, it looked like a wing sticking out of water. When I saw the fuselage reflecting through the water, I came right out of my seat with a shout.

"Yess!" I pumped my fist.

The plane lay in glacier runoff, in a V between two mountains, one wing angled up, and the fuselage covered by water. From previous satellite views it was clear that the plane had been under a glacier. At last it had melted enough to be exposed. It was so incredibly dreamlike to view, so fantastic, it was as if God were playing the ultimate story back to me, proving, once again that He was all in all.

From that point on, I felt pressed to go to Canada to examine the wreckage. Fall comes early in that country, with winter right behind. Then snow would bury it for another year. The window of time to get in there was closing so I was biting at the bit to go.

In looking over the picture, I surmised it was military because the wing was so drawn back. I'd flown in float planes, Beaver, Otter, Goose, helicopters, lots of commercial aircraft, and been to a few plane shows but had not seen any private airplanes with a wing that was angled back like that. If it were a fighter jet, the puzzling part was the length of its fuselage. It went into the water for a good distance. From the length of the fallen trees around it, I figured it had to be over thirty feet long. From the picture it appeared to be missing its nose, but there was a shinny object in the water maybe 100 feet ahead of it that might have been its nose. On second thought, what I surmised was a nose may have been its tail, lying underwater. I dismissed this because the shape would be backwards.

If it were a fighter jet, why hadn't the pilot pushed the ejector button and bailed? Considering this, I wondered if his parachute would've failed to fully open in that snow storm. Another thousand feet up that mountain there was an indentation in the rock, like an entrance to a cave. Maybe that was where the plane had crashed before sliding down to the bottom of that V. It was certainly steep enough country for that to have happened. If that plane had slammed head-on into that granite, it would have required a miracle for any flesh to survive. The more likely possibility was that the pilot circled the area before ejecting. But there was no end of speculation.

I wished I could remember the exact date of the crash. I figured I'd written it in my fishing log, but that book had been turned into the British Colombia Fisheries. The best I could surmise was January or February of 1985. I searched the internet for records of plane crashes in 1985, yet found none that was a match for January, February or even December of 1984. Canadian records were tougher to access so I had to make a call to government offices in BC and left a message, asking them if they had any records of a downed plane in late 1984, early 1985 along the coast, around Kemano.

A gal was kind enough to return my call to say there were no private planes that crashed in that area during said time. She advised I might want to check Canadian Military records. On August 22, 2017 I sent an email off to their military, describing the crash, asking them if they had any records that would be a match. On Jan. 16, 2018, I got an email from Rebecca Murray, at Library and Archives Canada stating, "*I have now completed my review with the consultation of various aircraft accident files, all dating from January and February 1985, most of which occurred in British Colombia. I noted the location of each accident and compared it on the map to Kemano to determine if it could have possibly been the accident you believed occurred there. I was not able to match any of the occurrences to the Kemano area. That said, please be assured that my review of our holdings has been thorough and diligent.*"

At that point, I was led to believe the plane was neither a private one nor a military one. The other options caused me to ponder.

Part of the problem with seeking records online was that the NSA observes what you are doing. I really didn't want military personnel reaching the plane before me. With my second book exposing the possibility of a piggish government during a time of chaos, I felt I was really under the NSA's eye after publishing it. I consider anyone who looks into my windows at night a pervert, and I feel the same way about anyone who sneaks through the backdoor of the internet and peeks in my emails. If they are illegally spying on us, they may be government and supposedly out to save us from ourselves, but I don't like it.

Friends suggested, 'What the government's really after is your treasure.'

Around this time I figured the plane story would be an easy trap for those government spies.

ITCHING TO GO BACK

I copied the satellite image of the plane crash and carried it around in my wallet. It was one story that was itching to be told; I wanted to tell the world about it because it proved that Tony and I did see the flare and did hear the aluminum door shut.

I told myself to keep quiet about the plane lest someone beat me to the crash site, but I could hardly contain myself. That Sunday, I saw a fellow who doesn't visit our church often but was always quite interesting. I ended up telling him the plane story but withholding where the bay was. He was onto it like a treasure hunter.

When I showed him the picture, he took a long look at it. "I bet that's the gold plane."

"What's the gold plane?"

"It's the plane that was a Federal Reserve shipment out of Seattle, heading east that just disappeared. I bet the pilots veered north instead. I bet that's it." He pointed at the fuselage, "I can see the fuselage there, going right down into the water. What's the name of the bay again?"

"I'm not telling."

"Are you going to head up there to find out what it is?"

"I'd like to, but I'm a little short on funds right now."

"I got a cousin who works a lot on the Slope up in Alaska. He's has plenty of money and a boat, too. If I gave him a ring, I bet he'd be happy to take you. But we need to know where it's at."

"I'll consider it."

His probing continued, "You need to take a metal detector with you, one that will work underwater because that plane has got no end of gold on it and you don't want to leave a bar behind." As he examined my little picture, the excitement in his eyes danced. There might've been a bit of greed too.

Realizing I wasn't telling him where the bay was, he asked, "Where is the nearest port?"

I steered away from that question.

Later, I considered his words and thought they had a good ring to them; Federal Reserve, gold, plane, crash. These words would work well in catching the eye of the NSA.

The following week two things perplexed me: I was on my laptop, searching the satellite imaging, inspecting the plane again. When I zoomed out, away from the crash site, I released my mouse, but for some reason it zoomed straight back in on the crash site. I was stunned to see this happen without me even touching the mouse. For a moment, it was as if I had no control over my computer.

At last I moved the mouse away from that bay, shifting the landscape into another region. I tested my mouse a number of times to see if it would repeat a zoom in on its own, but it wouldn't. In all the thousands of hours I've been on a computer, I've never before had that loss of control happen, not once.

The second thing I found suspicious, when I drove home from church and checked my emails on the same laptop, I noticed the computer hinge on one side wasn't working properly. On closer inspection it was missing a nut, which we later found on the floor. Had someone opened up the computer and in their hurry to put it back together knocked the tiny nut off the table? If someone had opened it, who was he, had something been inserted and why?

The strange thing about this was how complacency wove its way back into the routine. Even though I had an inkling that spies had invaded my house, my computer, only a few days passed before I went about everyday life as if nothing had happened. Underneath the surface, I think we fiction writers don't truly trust what we see at times because we spend so much time imagining stories.

Still, I felt I had a treasure in discovering that plane. I didn't place a whole lot of credence in the fantasy of it being some gold plane because the wing was angled back like a fighter jet. However, that week I showed the picture to another friend of mine at a coffee shop and didn't mention anything about gold.

When I finished, he scrutinized the picture and recommended, "You better go get the gold then."

I didn't know if all these Montanans had gold on their mind or what, but, after he said that, I wondered if the plane really did contain gold.

With September and snow coming in Canada, I was itching to get to the crash site even though I didn't have the money to go. I sent up a prayer and within two days we got a windfall on our vacation home rental that covered a trip. This was a real blessing, totally unexpected, out of the blue. My head was obsessed with heading back. I started seriously exploring various transportation methods to get there.

I received a quote for a charter boat to take me in from Kitimat, drop me off some 76 miles down the channel then pick me up a week later. That would cost $2,000.00 plus Canada's GST tax of 13%. A quote on a helicopter was $2,500.00 plus GST. A float plane was a bit less. After getting those quotes, I thought, rather than pay the Canadians and their GST, it would be just as cheap to buy a boat, drive it up there, then sell it after visiting the plane wreck. In Montana we don't pay sales tax.

While discussing a boat purchase, I heard the chirping of my wife. This entire adventure was too excessive when we had so many bills. Reluctantly, I gave my problems to God and decided to wait.

It wasn't long after a friend of mine, Jimmy, drove up from Nevada to be baptized. I'd met Jimmy years earlier at a neighbor's garden party. We easily hit it off because he used to man a crane on construction sites throughout Alaska. I'd visited him after I went skiing. He had that Alaskan hospitality that was always so welcoming. His cooking was great; and we swapped stories by the fire. Jimmy's been around and then some throughout Alaska and this country. I have good memories of the times spent listening to his adventures.

He eventually moved out of Montana and ended up in Nevada. He liked to travel and, now and again, we'd get a visit from him. But he was like a rare bird flying through. Thank God for texting.

When I received a call from him, I was surprised that he wanted to be baptized on his 74th birthday and wanted me to do it. I'd never baptized anyone before and wasn't sure if I was even legit to do it. I told him my concerns and suggested that my pastor baptize him. But he didn't know my pastor and insisted I do it. Wouldn't it be something if all humanity were beating down your door to be baptized?

Before we walked down to the river I fed him breakfast and showed him the picture of the plane sticking out of the water. I'd be lying if I hadn't hoped he'd be interested in my adventure.

I suggested, "I was thinking about buying a boat, get one on Craig's List or something, then maybe sell it after. What do you think about a trip up there?"

"I'm in no shape to go up and down those mountains. They look pretty steep."

I couldn't blame him. From the topographical map it was obviously a hump. I figured that was the end of my adventure with Jimmy.

September hit, and it was looking like I wouldn't make it back to the British Colombia coast before the snow flew. I figured if I was going to swim in that water, I had to leave by the end of the month. The glaciers above the plane weren't completely melted off but were at their lowest by then. Deep down I had a real longing to go and see if that pilot made it, but we just didn't have that kind of money to be running around on some remote adventure.

The first weekend in September, I sent up this really farfetched prayer that was more of a flowery dream than a prayer, "Lord, it would be fun if You provided a boat to go to Canada with a guy to go along who had lots of money." I chuckled when I finished the prayer because it seemed so unrealistic. "Oh, and by the way, it would be good, too, if he had a metal detector that would work underwater."

While I prayed I had a sense that God had just awakened, rubbed his nose with a bit of a yawn, then said, "I have just the man who'll provide all you need. Don't worry about it."

That reaction seemed so farfetched it was like an

illusion, darn near laughable, but I had to believe that He was orchestrating all of this because He'd hidden the plane for so long.

The next day I got a call from Jimmy.

It wasn't long before he said, "I've been thinking about that plane story you told me, and I was thinking I'll go buy a boat to go up there. I've wanted a boat anyway. What do you think of me going with you?"

"Like to Canada?"

"Yeah, I can buy the boat."

I knew he was an adventurer, but his call came right off the page. As he carried on, I was taken aback at how gung-ho he was. But I acted like I was hard to get and asked, "You wouldn't have a metal detector, would you?"

"Yes, I've got this real good one that I traded for."

"Does it work underwater?"

"That's what it's for. It's all waterproof."

It wasn't but two days later that he was standing at my doorstep, chomping at the bit to get rolling. I mean you could feel his rush to get underway.

I wasn't in such a hurry because I'd been watching the weather report up in Kitimat, and it was rain for the entire week. What's ironic was, the day after he called, he left his place and, in his haste, he forgot the metal detector.

He felt badly about it and I should've kept my mouth shut but joked, "Without that metal detector, how're we going to retrieve all that gold?"

I could see his wheels turning as he walked around.

"I'll go get it."

"No, you don't. You must have a neighbor or someone who can send it up?"

"You're not traveling all the way back there just to get a metal detector. That's over 800 miles."

"Don't worry about it." Jimmy has a way about him that once he makes up his mind, that's it.

Before he left, he handed me a thick envelope, "There's $4,000.00 cash there and I'll give you a check for another two thousand to go buy the boat."

"I want to get some skin in this game and I planned on spending at least two thousand so you keep your check."

When I took his cash I knew the adventure was on. He headed back to Nevada to get the metal detector, and the next day I headed off to Spokane to get the boat.

The trip

There is no doubt that Jimmy likes to drive. Maybe that came from spending one day too long in a crane up under the cold, dark, Alaska winter sky, locked into working for months on end.

He actually made it back to Montana before I brought the boat back from Spokane. The rest of the trip was like a whirlwind to get up to Canada. I felt as if we were being pushed by the heavens to get there. When I'd searched Craig's List for a boat, I also looked for an inflatable dingy to use to get to shore. I found one but I couldn't catch up with its owner. I assumed it wasn't a big deal because Jimmy said he wasn't going to climb that mountain, so I assumed he'd drop me off on shore and I'd go up by myself. But I brought my wetsuit just in case he wanted to go up, then I could drop him off on shore, anchor and swim back. I hadn't worn that wetsuit in fifteen years. I made lots of assumptions.

We left on a Wednesday evening and crossed the border around 10:30 pm. Having about 1000 miles to go, Jimmy wanted to travel all night. I had to bend his ear to pull over for us to sleep. We slept in the back of his truck.

Banff and Jasper were picturesque, their mountains rising sky high. I don't think Jimmy even noticed those big mountains; he was locked into the road, driving. He said he'd traveled that road many times heading up to Alaska. It was evident. I'd never seen a 74 year old with so much drive to get somewhere. Even at his age, he was a monster for traveling and where I was cautious going downhill, towing a boat, he never thought twice about giving it gas.

I found the Canadian road system incredibly well kept. For their population, about California's population, they did a great job on their roads.

Friday morning, we made it into Terrace. I was amazed to see what had happened to that town since I'd been there last. There were a lot of new buildings. They even had a Wal-Mart. We had breakfast at Denny's.

Something didn't sit well with Jimmy at Denny's because he needed to stay close to a bathroom afterwards.

When we drove by Onion Lake I recalled the night I had pulled out of Kitimat, eons ago. The memory of that snowy night was so fresh because I had pulled into a lone gas station that sat out in the middle of nowhere, between Kitimat and Terrace. I'd never gone to that gas station before. It was well past its prime back in 1985 and only had two pumps. That snowy night, while I was filling up, another vehicle pulled in and the guy ended up on the opposite side of the gas pump. In the falling snow we struck up a conversation and I found it ironic that after so many years away from Kitimat, he was coming back the same night that I was leaving for California.

I recalled him grinning when he said, "Life's a circle isn't it?"

He was twenty years my senior and I figured he knew more about life than I did. His comment resonated for me and I thought of it as I traveled the long road to Prince Rupert to catch the ferry south to the States.

When I drove by the Onion Lake area with Jimmy,

I didn't notice that gas station. Perhaps it had been torn down. When I think of the man's comment on that snowy night, I no longer see life as a circle but a straight line, aimed straight at the return of Christ. Romans 8:22 speaks of the pains of childbirth. Could those pains increase with wars the closer we get to His return?

I'm amazed at how fast life's ride is. Wasn't it yesterday that Louis and Clark came west? Isn't it amazing how fast civilization has progressed in the past 100 years? Like it or not, all nations have been pushed into the modern age, all locked into this ride. From jungle natives to Arctic natives, this world is zooming toward 5 G. There's no escaping it.

Dan. 12:4 "But you, Daniel, shut up the words, and seal the book until the time of the end: many shall run to and fro, and knowledge shall increase." Interestingly, it doesn't say *wisdom* shall increase but knowledge. With the internet, hasn't knowledge increased exponentially?

By noon we were in Kitimat. It had been thirty-odd years since I'd been back but it seemed like yesterday. How time had flown. I sat up like a child in Disneyland, wide-eyed at every corner. Having lived in that rainy town for eight years, I was saying, "Wow! Wow! Wow!"

Maybe it was the fact that the sun had broken through, but the town seemed so fresh, new and lively. Despite new buildings, I was surprised that the population had shrunk from 12,000 to 9,000.

We drove into the town's center to do some shopping. I bought more fishing gear and vegetables. What I was not used to were the high prices in Canada. Though you get almost 20% benefit from the exchange rate, it doesn't compensate for their prices which are double or more. A small camping propane tank worth $3.79 in the states was on sale for $11.99 in Kitimat. Then add to that their tax of 13% and you really started feeling like you were in a socialistic country.

Jimmy kept saying, "I don't know how these people can afford to buy anything."

We made it down to the MK marina and, because of the outgoing tide, I was in a hurry to get underway, haphazardly tossing our stuff into the boat. Kemano's dock was 66 miles away and we needed to get there before dark.

Jimmy was more cautious and I don't doubt our visit to Denny's had something to do with it. He still looked green about the gills.

When I fired up the boat I noticed the RPM gauge wasn't registering. I found out later that its wire had slipped off. I also noticed the alternator reading wasn't in positive territory. This could've been a disaster had I not run across another boater who was kind enough to test it for us. Thankfully it was charging fine. In examining it, we found a crack in an adjusting bar that held the alternator so we went back to Kitimat to see if we could get it welded. It was near 5:00 pm when we arrived and I thought we'd be lucky to catch anyone at that time on a Friday.

I was praying and thankfully we found a fellow at Bravo's welding. With the high price of everything, I prayed his services wouldn't cost more than $50.00. The welder found out where we were from and didn't charge us a thing. May God Bless him.

We sped back to the dock and put the adjusting bar and alternator back together. To say that I was in a hurry to get rolling before dark was an understatement. The only problem I saw with the boat was the steering which was incredibly stiff. I bumped the dock a few times just getting out of the marina.

At last, I took Jimmy for a spin. It was a bit choppy.

He wasn't on that boat for five minutes before he said, "I got a bad feeling about this boat."

From his stark look, I could see that he was truly fearful about the craft. Odd, because I thought it was running good. Though the steering was stiff, it was running better than any small craft I'd been on. I encouraged him to hang in there just a bit and motored closer to shore before slowing down to a troll.

"What do you think now, Jimmy?"

He looked worried, saying, "I got a bad feeling about this boat."

"But it's running good." There was a bit of a chop but it wasn't bad. I wondered if his breakfast at Denny's was still giving him problems.

"What we need to do is go back and organize everything." He was pale as he looked toward shore.

I could see that he was nervous. "Jimmy, even if we had it all organized would you be okay on this boat?"

"No, I've got a bad feeling about this boat. And I've been on a lot of boats in some severe weather, too." As he looked to shore, his eyes told stories of distant harbors and storms, "This boat scares me."

"If that's the case, do you mind if I take off by myself?"

"Yeah, you go ahead."

"I can take you to a friend of mine in Kitimat who'd look after you, take you fishing. Terry's a good guy."

"No, don't worry about me."

"You'd like Terry. He really knows river fishing. He'd take you out. You could stay at his place."

"No, don't worry about me."

Though the tide was in my favor the sun wasn't so, when we got back to the dock, I hurried to get Jimmy settled in. We started taking his stuff off the boat. It was disturbing to see his flashlight go. I hadn't brought my big one because he'd brought his. I was disappointed to see it hauled off, but told myself it'd be okay because I knew I had a little one around somewhere.

In looking back there are a lot of things I should've done differently. I wished I had reorganized my stuff and found that light because I really needed it later; the same with some raingear and a coat that I thought were on board but weren't. Strange how pushed I felt to get out of there, cruise down that channel. Undoubtedly, this had to do with the twenty foot tides, plus it was a clear day, no rain which was rare in that country. As I said, time wasn't on my side. I felt like I had a monkey on my back and, as soon as Jimmy's stuff was off the boat, I was powering down the channel.

It wasn't long before I noticed something disturbing; I was using more fuel than anticipated. This put an edge on the trip. As I glanced back at my three, five gallon extra tanks, they suddenly didn't seem sufficient. I kept on but started to consider my options.

When I entered Gardner channel, I saw the fuel tank was less than ¾ full. This wasn't good. Ahead was the first and only moving boat I saw that evening. I aimed for it, slowed and, when I drew near, waved.

Europa was its name. They were ferrying a truck back from either the logging camp or Kemano.

We had a little chat about location before I asked, "Do you have any extra fuel I can purchase?"

The older, bigger man replied, "I'm afraid not; this rig's a diesel. Where're you heading?"

"Kemano."

"What are you doing up here?"

"I used to commercial fish this channel, thirty-two years ago."

"I used to commercial fish salmon on the Queen Charlotte Islands." He thumbed up the channel. "You might be able to get gas in Kemano or the logging outfit."

"You think I can get it there?"

"Yeah, those guys will probably help you out."

Considering how friendly the guys at Kemano had been in the past, I decided to throw caution to the wind and power on.

Half an hour later the sun dropped over the mountains. Though it was still light out, shadows were cast straight across the channel. The fear around dusk was hitting a drifting log. That channel was an active logging area and those loggers didn't always get every stick that dropped into the water. Additionally, the window I was gazing through wasn't the clearest and the wiper didn't work.

With light fading, I sat up pert, searching for any drifting wood. Still, I couldn't see that far ahead. When I spotted some, it was almost too late to veer away. A stretch where riptide was occurring proved to be challenging, steering through a minefield of driftwood.

While fun fishing with Elaine, in our distant past, we were traveling back a bit late one evening and hit a log going full blast. Amazingly, the 19 foot boat flew straight over it and powered on. God had to be looking after us because I've heard stories of the same scenario playing out and the boat's drive leg being ripped right off. You'd be crab bait then.

Strangely, I liked being by myself in that desolate channel. It was peculiar because there was a lonesomeness in that remote area that should've put me on edge. It came with a bit of what-next thrill. Shadowing me were fuel concerns, but I liked how it made me lean into my Maker, my Christ. He'd gotten me that far and I knew He was faithful to take me the distance.

Following Christ is really an easy one once you figure out that God isn't some cruel taskmaster. In fact His yoke is easy and His burden is light. There is also an aspect of the cross that is incredibly mysterious. Though it was the cruelest killing device of its time, where birds of prey would be working on a sufferer, picking at him before he was dead, it holds incredible glory and life. Christ tells us to die to self for a reason. Why, because he knows that at the end of self all you have is self. Whereas with Him, if we give up our lives for His way, His direction, for His love, for His path, then we get a life that was made for us by Him, by the author of life. In the end it is the difference between life and death, having something incredibly grand rather than holding onto something that causes shame and plainly stinks. In short, we aren't smart enough to run our own lives.

Once you really trust and obey Him, it's crazy how alive life is, which makes you more willing to take up your cross. Truly, He knows what's best for us.

I've always liked those times in life where it's just Him and me. I'm very thankful that He trusts me enough to stretch me out of my comfort zone during those times.

The channel started to narrow with rock walls rising vertically from the channel then angling upwards. I felt incredibly small. It was amazing to see God's creative hand. This landscape was so rough and tough it reminded me of Him. The Bible said He named all the stars. Aren't there over a billion stars?

I once saw a picture of the earth taken from the

Voyager space craft. I don't know how many billion miles away from the earth the picture was taken, but earth was so small, such a tiny dot, that, if it weren't for a sliver of light somehow exposing it and a computer curser pointing it out, I would've never noticed. That was our dinky, dinky, dust of a planet. I considered that and the dinky, dinky humans that ran around trying to figure everything out. And here this dinky, dinky creature called, "man," was trying to figure out God!!!

I wondered what God thought about all the theologians and professors who tried to put Him in their dinky, dinky box? Was He amused by them? If they were not in relationship with Him, did He look at them as just one of the 7 billion?

Humans are a worrisome creature. We worry so much about things that never happen. And I'm no different. I like Christ's instructions about worrying, telling us not to. Would God have had less work or fretting about counting the hairs on our head than naming the billion planets? And here He came to our dinky, dinky, planet and took on the form of man, submitted himself to mankind to show His love for us. What an amazing God!

He is incredibly intimate and I saw His hand in the greenery and landscape of Gardner Channel. Considering how deep that channel was, I admired God's vastness.

Miles went under my keel, and with the sun fading, the cool of evening fell. I was getting cold but held my course. Coming around one bend, I saw the lights of the lone logging operation tucked into a cove on my starboard side. Its presence was reassuring.

Concerned about not making it to Kemano before dark, I headed for the lights of the logging camp, thinking I could tie up there for the night. But not far into this change of course I wondered if I'd be intruding on them. Unsure, I veered off and continued toward Kemano.

I figured it was less than five miles. Coming around the next corner, I don't know if the mountains suddenly rose or the darkness suddenly fell, but the abruptness of black darkness caught me off guard. Though the chart was sitting on my lap, it did me no good as it was too dark to read it. This was where my flashlight would've come in handy, if I could have found it. Good thing I was buzzing around the next point by then. A few miles ahead were the lights of Kemano. How encouraging.

Their lights reflected off the water, stretching across the bay, beckoning, inviting me toward them. As I approached, I slowed, really wishing I had my flashlight. I recalled something about the depth near Kemano, but wasn't exactly sure what. Suspicious that the water level wasn't that deep on the side, I slowed down and thought I'd be safe from bottoming out if I followed their lights. It was a good thing I was puttering because I couldn't see this shoreline suddenly appear on my portside.

When the Mercury leg touched bottom, what a panic! Good grief what a panic! Powering the leg up, I turned off the engine and prayed, "Please help me Lord. Please Jesus, please help me out of this area."

Jimmy had been right about us not being prepared – if I could only find my flashlight. God had mercy and I was able to get that kicker started and back out of there. Thank God, there was only minor damage to the propeller.

THE DREAM

oming off an adrenaline rush, I puttered into
Kemano's dock. It was totally different from what I'd
remembered. Their yacht club dock was gone. The
few boats remaining were commercial. The other dock that
we used to tie up to was gone. I tied up to a dock I hadn't
seen before. Low tide was underway and the gangways
leading down to the two docks were at a steep angle. Other
than the lights the place looked abandoned.

When I noticed how wet and sodden the wood was, I
realized I didn't miss the B.C. rain. The dock appeared to
be melting into the water. Still, I felt incredibly blessed to
have made it to Kemano six days after Jimmy had called. It
was unreal.

I began digging out cooking gear when I heard someone
say, "Ohhh wha iaaa," and some more gibberish at the other
dock.

I didn't understand their words, but they sounded
playful so I poked my head outside the boat, calling out,
"Hello." I peered through the dark, toward the docks on
the far side. There were some more sounds from over there
but I couldn't make any words out. Either they were joking
with me or drunk.

Curious to see who they were, I hopped out of the boat
and hustled up the steep gangway. The covered gangway

was the only dry area around. It was lit. Near the shore, I heard some shuffling, coming from a garbage can. Gazing into the garbage can, I saw some mice that were hopping straight in the air, trying to get out. The can was too tall for them. I was amazed that they could leap straight up, over fifteen inches.

I walked to shore, heading for the talkers. When I heard some snarling growls along with the gibberish, I knew who I was dealing with at the other end of the dock. Gravel crunched under my boots as I approached. The talking halted, and I heard some splashes. Sea lions were hopping off the dock.

Needing a bathroom, I searched the buildings. There were a handful of them, mostly small and all locked tighter than a bank. If those buildings hadn't had aluminum siding, they would have melted away like everything else in that rainy place.

Years ago, when I'd worked in Kemano, one of the jobs we did was a concrete pour atop a slab that housed large fuel tanks. Wanting to see how it performed, I strolled in that direction only to be met by one huge stack of twisted metal. I was surprised to see the area where they stored the fuel tanks was all torn down. How the hand of time had played. Memories flooded back. I recalled going to the Kemano dump with my construction buddies. The dump was out in the sticks and had a number of bears, both black and grizzly. When I hopped out to get rid of some garbage, one of my buddies was "kind enough" to lock the truck's door. Black bears are generally intimidated by humans, but grizzlies are not. One of the 200 lbs cubs sized me up as it sauntered toward me. Since the guys liked the game, I had to leap in the back of the truck to save my hide. My good buddies had a laugh on that one.

Aware of grizzlies, I found my way back to the boat. I banged around at the dock, making my supper. It was nice to have the towering lights behind me, and it was nice to feel the warmth of the propane stove as corn on the cob, potatoes and beets, boiled away. I'd forgotten to buy butter but it turned into a great supper when I found Jimmy's coconut oil.

It had been many years since I'd slept on a boat. Moving my bedding around, I happily snuggled into the sleeping bag. While lying there, I thought of the chances of getting off that shelf that I had hit. Sometimes in life, when I look back, I see a lot of God's hand.

With the slight rock of the boat, and soothing lap of water, it wasn't long before sleep embraced me. I'd forgotten how that old friend had hung around boats.

Somewhere in the night the boat abruptly jerked back and forth. Unexpectedly awakened, I sat up, and listened. The dock was lit and I saw the silhouette of a sea lion's head that reflected off the back wall of the cubby. It was gazing through the cubby's glass at the back of my head. This reflection was on a white wall and the movement of the sea lion was like watching some Alfred Hitchcock, "The Birds," movie. It was downright spooky.

I called out, "Hey!" and struggled out of the sleeping bag, hurrying to get my hands on a fishing knife, air horn and bear spray before poking my head outside the boat. The sea lion had vanished. When I went back to bed, I set those protective treasures right next to me and my ears were alert to any sounds.

Though I heard movement up on the dock again, I was thankful to fall asleep.

I don't have a clue what time it was when I abruptly awoke. A dream was before me – one of those foretelling dreams. I was gazing at the very end of Chief Mathews Bay in a night scene. Halfway up were two enormous cannons, half the size of the mountain; one cannon was white, the other black. Both cannons faced east, toward Kemano. Interestingly, the design of these cannons looked contemporary, as if they'd been designed by Apple computer. The cannons stood right next to each other like they had been set on weigh scales. At the close of that vision there was a unique red *Warning* and a symbol that I was unfamiliar with. It looked like the coat of a highway flag person although its reflective red boxes and lines spoke of something more detailed. What most surprised me was a symbol of a snake in the middle of it.

My first thought was war was coming and from the size of the cannons it was going to be a big one. My second thought was Elaine would have fun with this one; she was my vision/dream interpreter. At the same time I was aware of a strong sense of completion, as if I'd been given a gift, as if that had been the purpose of this trip.

I dismissed this notion. Why would that be true if I hadn't seen the plane yet, especially if it had gold?

An Old Friend

The following morning was a beauty, blue sky, brisk, with fall in the air. I banged away, making breakfast. Jimmy had packed some Spam for the trip, and I was glad I ended up with some because it blended well with the leftovers from the night before. The smell of fried onions drifted up in the misty air. Makes me hungry just recalling it.

It was refreshing to power away from Kemano harbor on a calm sea. It seemed like only yesterday that the guys were trying to get The Four Seasons off the dock in the dead of winter with a fierce wind coming down on us.

Glancing back at the dock, I was flooded with more memories of working in construction there, and the day when we had gone water skiing. Though it was in late summer, I'll never forget how chilly that water was. It was so cold that I decided to have the boat pull me off the dock instead of dragging me out of the water. I had some free line going and let the boat power up before I jumped off the dock. I had never done it before, only seen others do it. Amazingly, it worked, and I skied right out into that channel. The biggest thrill, however, was after I had taken a tumble and was waiting for the boat to come around – a sea lion spotted me then disappeared underwater. A minute passed, and its head popped up fifty yards closer. It looked directly at me then slipped its head under, disappearing. A few minutes later it popped up another fifty yards closer. My fear was it might take a bite out of me before the boat dragged me out of there. Not a silly fear, this actually happened in Endurance, Shackleton's Incredible Voyage. A sea leopard (not sure if this is the same as our sea lion) chased a man, swimming under the ice only to pop up further. Then slid up on the ice and chased the man. It was all the man could do to escape.

That September morning, as I powered into Chief Mathews Bay, I felt like I had come back to an old friend. Maybe it was how the sky played, clouds drifting over, covering up some of the blue. Below this canopy lay a dead calm bay. It was exhilarating to cruise over its glassy surface. This bay was so pure, so unspoiled.

Generally when I have gone back to check out an old school or something, they seem so much smaller than I remembered but Chief Mathews was just the opposite; it appeared much bigger than I remembered. I could understand why, in years past, we had stayed in there looking for that pilot, and fishing for more time than normal. The boat sped nicely past the main waterfalls on the right.

I had the chart sitting on my lap and constantly studied it to pick up waypoints. What was perplexing was not being able to really lock in some of the waypoints with the chart. Was I at this spot or farther on? After having looked at the images on Google Earth for so long it should have been obvious, but it wasn't. I motored along the shore, almost to its end, and then crossed over to where I figured we were the night we spotted the flare. Then I motored over to the area where I had heard the aluminum door shut. That area didn't look like I remembered it. Maybe it was the fact that there was no snow but I couldn't pinpoint whether it had been on one side of a certain jut-out or the other. Either way, there were only a hundred or so yards that separated them. That was encouraging. The deciding factor was which one offered better anchorage.

Examining the area, I calculated how I'd do a three point anchoring system. Without a dinghy or Jimmy to drop me off, I was going to have to swim to shore. That was no mystery. But first I had to make sure my anchoring was sound, as it wouldn't be good to return to a boat that had broken its lines or was overturned. I could've gone with a conventional anchor down at the end of the bay, where it was shallower, but it would be a long swim to shore and an even longer hike up that mountain.

The shoreline was pretty much vertical on two sides with rock walls rising straight out of the water. The other side of this anchorage was a mixture of sand and rock that nicely angled away from the main shore, making it a natural point to string a line. I figured, after securing my ropes, I'd have to go through two tidal cycles, twelve hours, just to check my lines. Twenty feet of tidal action is nothing to fool with.

I decided to do a bit of fishing so I trolled across to the other side. I had to go there anyway to get a better view of the mountain I was intending to climb. Some of that area is so steep if you made the wrong turn going up you'd have to backtrack before ascending again. Wanting to avoid that, I took the afternoon to plan a path up the mountain. The misting, gathering clouds, made it difficult. The weather never got any clearer either. Those clouds always hung low.

Near some waterfalls, I saw my fishing pole jerk. With a yank, I freed the line from the downrigger and reeled in a rock cod, a dark brown beauty. With glee, I scaled and filleted it. I did some mooching in that area but to no avail.

Early afternoon, I motored the craft toward the middle of the bay before having a nap. It started to sprinkle.

Not giving up
her secrets easily

Before the sun dropped, I motored back to where I intended to anchor and started the process of tying off. On one side I tied my line to a tree. This line was 100ft and I put a buoy on it, leaving it floating. I then motored to the opposite shore; hopped off the bow and quickly tied a rope to a dead fall, but then spotted a few big rocks and decided to use them instead.

In the six minutes it took me to untie my line from that dead fall and retie it around those rocks, then go back to push the boat out – it wouldn't budge! The dissipating tide had run out that fast. With all my might I was unable to lift the bow to push it out, could not budge that boat. Panicked, I hopped back on deck, hustled to get it started, rammed it in reverse, praying to beat the band. Thank God it came off that spot because the rocky area underneath was unforgiving. Had it settled, my drive could've been damaged.

I drove out deeper to drop the anchor off the bow, then dragged it toward shore. To complete the three point anchoring, I attached one line to my stern on my portside and the other line to my starboard. The boat's position was forty feet off that rock wall where the landscape towered nearly straight up.

Darkness fell, and it started to rain hard. I cooked up half the rock cod. Fresh fish is so good. I had it along with leftover potatoes, onions, beets and Jimmy's coconut oil – yummy.

That day, while rumbling through my stuff I found my flashlight. Thank God. On occasion, I checked my position, flashing the light toward the rock wall, then to the portside and starboard side. As the tide went out I saw the bones of tree branches underwater. They rose in the water surprisingly close.

The drum of rain beating onto the deck went along with my washing of the cooking wares. On occasion, water would make it through the canvas cover and drip onto the beam's shelf. Conscious of the heavy moisture, I moved the pack of stick matches into a storage bin in the cubby. With the back portion of the boat exposed to the rains, I hoped that the bilge pump wouldn't drain the batteries.

I melted into my sleeping bag and listened to the continual drum of rain on the aluminum. Again, I quickly fell asleep.

Somewhere in the night I awoke and got up to check the boat's position. The tide looked quite low and I had to adjust the lines about ten feet as some sunken tree branches appeared right under the boat. Then I went back to bed.

Later, I awoke to check the lines. It was dark and rainy as before, but the tide was rising and the distance to the back rock wall was closer, thirty feet or so away. Concerned, I shimmied along the starboard side in my bare legs to check the anchor line. It was fine. I knew I had to get it right because there'd be no possibility of adjustments once I went up that mountain.

It was great to get out of the rain, back into the warm sleeping bag. Laying there, I listened to the incessant drumming. Though I tried to sleep, my thoughts went to the plane up the mountain. I really didn't want to see any 32 year old remains of that pilot at the crash site. It would have been so good if the helicopter had actually rescued him and he'd lived to have a family and a good life. It didn't matter to me then if the helicopter pilot were lying to me to keep some military secret hush-hush. I really didn't want to find any sign that the pilot had died at the plane crash.

The rain continued through the morning which made a dreary, heavy morning. The cold seeped into me. Maybe it was the 50 degree weather or the continual rain or having to get up so many times at night, but the dampness had gotten me. When I looked over to shore some forty feet away, then realized the steepness of that mountain I had to climb, the crash site started to feel like a thousand miles away. Would I be able to swim to shore, go up the mountain, swim around the plane, taking pictures, then come down the mountain and swim back to the boat, without cramping up? If I cramped up, would I be able to make it back? That was my fear.

I figured if I had breakfast I'd feel better, but when I opened a sealed container of vitamins and found that they, too, had gotten damp, I started to wonder. The air was so damp that the box of wooden matches which I had placed in a dry storage bin in the cubby wouldn't light. Thankfully, I had a butane lighter, but it, too, barely started. I didn't know if it was about out of gas, or the dampness had gotten it, but it would not hold a flame. After about the tenth click, I became nervous and said a prayer. Finally, it managed to light the camp stove. Thank God.

My wheels were working over the possibility of not being able to start a fire after spending the rainy day, hiking up the mountain, pouring out my energy at the plane site, then down the mountain and swimming again to the boat. I'm in decent shape, but not a triathlon athlete. Those waters were Canadian cold.

Having had hypothermia in the past, I had some warning signals flashing. Another flash was the rope that I had used on my portside wasn't that sound. I didn't like seeing it rub against the rock all day as the tides went up and down. It might have been fine, but if it broke it would be a tragedy.

As I ate breakfast, the rain continued, pounding away on the canvas cover. I considered the magnesium fire starter, which was still in its package. I had never tried one of those in such wet conditions. Everything was under some hazy gloom. It cast hopelessness. Would that magnesium starter even work in this damp air? I tipped my head back to take in the tall trees, stretching up the side of the mountain. It was so steep I couldn't see any landscape beyond the tree tops. At their bases nestled ferns and dark green moss. The continuing downpour was relentless. Yet, I told myself I needed to buckle down and take the plunge.

Somewhere in this mental battle an older man showed up. He didn't want to buckle down and take the plunge. Maybe if I had gotten in the wetsuit I would've been more gung-ho, but, being cold, I just wasn't gung-ho about doing anything. That wetsuit was so constrictive anyway; it was difficult to pull on and if my muscles cramped up it would be impossible to take off. In this mental battle to mount up, the Labrador retriever in me just took off. I don't know where he went, but I wasn't going to swim to shore when I wasn't sure I could start a fire on my return. Nor was I willing to hang out there, waiting for the weather to clear if I couldn't cook a hot meal that night. Who knew when the weather would clear? I've seen it rain in that country for three months straight.

Gazing at that rock wall, I felt like a failure. I was within a mile of the plane, yet not up that mountain. Such was my predicament. I was terribly disappointed, but I knew it wasn't safe. It would have been different if I'd had one more person with me. If I had to do it all over again, I would not have stopped at that Denny's restaurant. I've had a lot of great meals at various Denny's, and good ones, but Jimmy had been struck by something there. I needed Jimmy.

It was good to fire up the boat, hear it rumble and see water jet out the stern from the bilge pump. From the length of time it flowed, I could see I should've pumped it earlier. It was also good to gather up my anchor lines and power on out of there.

Rain, rain, British Colombia could have it. Needing fuel, I headed back to Kemano to see if I could purchase some. As I cruised around the point, I cast my last look of Chief Mathews Bay. Except for the wake the boat made, the surface was dead calm.

PETRO

Nearing Kemano, I viewed the shoreline on my portside where my prop had hit bottom the other night. Strange to think that the entire trip could've ended there. It could've also ended in Chief Mathews had I not been able to get the boat off the shore when the tide went out.

After docking in Kemano, I heard a truck so I hustled up the gangway to get to shore. One of Alcan's guys appeared and asked what I was doing there. I told him the plane story then asked him if I could buy fuel. He gave me a wary eye with one of those – *I've heard it all before* – attitudes and made some comment that everyone was stealing everything from them and they hardly had any fuel for themselves. Weird to think anyone even ended up at their remote dock let alone stole from them as their big tanks were all scrapped out.

He ended up radioing to town and told me, "Wait in your boat, there'll be another representative down."

Though he seemed negative, I remained optimistic that they'd help.

Half an hour later a guy came down the gangway. He looked maybe in his early thirties, appeared right out of a washing machine, in a navy blue company coat and pants.

"We can't help you on your fuel; we don't sell gas. But I can radio Sea Tack for you."

His first comment took me back. "That would probably cost thousands for them to come down here. I'm only looking for ten gallons."

He was unmoved. "What are you doing way out here?"

I told him the plane story, making sure I hit on the point that we thought the flare had come from one of their guys, hoping to draw some gas credit sympathy.

He remained indifferent.

I pointed at the old aluminum ferry boat tied to the dock, insides all gutted out. "Is that the old Nechako?"

He nodded. "Yes."

I told him that I had worked in construction in Kemano and asked how many people ran the plant now.

"We're down to about fifteen."

"You're kidding. Weren't there over two hundred before?"

"About a hundred and fifty."

I talked to him about Kitimat. As we talked, a sizable grizzly walked by on the riprap near the water's edge. The bear was quite impressive, no more than forty feet away. Interestingly, it didn't even look our way. Thankfully the dock separated him from us.

In viewing this young man, I wondered if I knew his parents. He had the olive skin color of the Portuguese and, back in the day, I had a lot of Portuguese friends in Kitimat. As far as that goes, he could've been Tony's son if Tony ever got married. I asked him if he knew if the church I used to go to was still there.

"Yes, life hasn't changed that much." He gazed at my boat. "How long have you had your boat?"

"Not even a week, we bought it in Idaho on Tuesday."

"Ah yes." He grinned at it. "The perils of boating."

I had to chuckle at this kid's lack of compassion. It was obvious he was not going to be generous with his company's fuel. Rio Tinto Mining clearly wasn't the Alcan of old. The Alcan of the past would've helped me in a heartbeat.

It was amazing how happy he appeared. "We don't see too many boats out this way anymore."

I plowed on. It was good to get away from there. With half a tank of fuel, I reasoned, maybe . . . just maybe. Another ten or so miles went under my keel and with the last of civilization behind me, and the fuel gauge sinking to ¼ tank, I was feeling the pinch. The writing was clearly on the wall: without another ten gallons, I was not going to make it back to Kitimat. I prayed and my heart felt heavy. I'd been traveling for a half hour yet not seen one boat. And boy, did I pray.

Cutting through a long stretch, I stared at a point in the distance. The channel curved there and I couldn't see beyond it. When you're out in the wilderness, life is, incredibly real when you're running on empty and there's no gas station. I am not the kind of person who runs out of fuel. In fact I can't recall ever running out of fuel. I knew my Redeemer lived, and I just didn't see Him taking me all the way there and leaving me. Deep down it was as if I were mourning. I was desperate for His help. This was truly a stretch of faith, but I knew He lived.

Ahead, I thought I saw movement, yes, a boat appeared. It was moving fast. Behind it was another. I wondered if it was in tow.

I headed for them. A mile later we all slowed. The boat behind veered off. It was a small jet boat. Both boats looked brand new.

The larger boat came in on my portside. As we neared, a window opened and the captain, another thirties looking character, poked his head out. We did the cordials before I asked if he had any extra fuel I could purchase.

"I can't help you. The last time we were out, we barely made it back with only twenty-five gallons to spare." Everything about this youngish captain was professional, his hair recently styled, his camo clothing appeared just off the racks.

"I understand," I replied, feeling heat come to my face.

Near the stern an older deck hand placed a buoy between our two boats.

The youngish captain gazed at my Idaho boat tags. "You're a long way from home."

I nodded, trying to hide my downcast feeling with a pleasant face. I probably looked lost.

The captain disappeared inside the cabin then reappeared, coming through the wheelhouse door, his arm trailing back toward the open cabin. "But meet your country woman."

A woman stepped out on deck. I'd guess she was in her fifties. In camo gear, she looked quite pleasant.

"Hi there," I did my best to give her a welcoming grin, "Where you from?"

"Utah. Where are you from?"

"Montana."

"I was born in Montana," she replied, naming the town.

It must've been a small town out east because I didn't recall it. "What are you doing here?"

"I came to hunt grizzly."

"Great!" I hoped she'd get one, thumbing back. "I just saw a nice one in Kemano. It was real close, walking along the shore, just the other side of the docks. I bet it was over six hundred pounds. Can I ask what do you do for a living?"

"I've worked in the parks services in Utah."

"Cool."

She looked as if she were getting cold and quietly said something to the captain before disappearing back in the cabin. There was a chilly sprinkle.

He asked, "What are you doing way out here?"

"Thirty-two years ago I used to commercial fish in this channel. We went after prawns. . ." I rattled on and began to tell him the plane story.

Seconds later his first mate passed a five gallon jug of gas over. My heart lept at the sight and I didn't waste time filling my empty five gallon jug.

Somewhere in my story of putting the Coast Guard captain on notice, I handed the empty back to the deckhand. I didn't know how generous the captain was going to be with his fuel but I wasn't going to say that I needed another five gallons. God knew I needed it, I figured He could do the nudging.

"It's too bad Rio Tinto didn't help you out," said the captain.

"I know, and back in the day, I went into Kemano twice because I thought it was their man who'd shot that flare." I turned away to move the tank I just filled. When I turned back, there was the second offering sitting on the side of the boat. My eyes lit up at the sight. Wow!

The stylish captain wore a pair of camo cutoffs and pranced about to keep warm, his arms held tight across his chest.

I was so out of style it wasn't funny. My blue pair of pants were at least twenty years old, and my dull green nylon insulated Army vest was so worn the padding was showing.

As I filled another five gallon tank, I finished the plane story.

Still prancing about to stay warm, the captain added, "I'm a pilot too."

"What do you fly?"

"Helicopter, I purchased a Bell 206 last year."

I sent an approving glance over his boat, everything looked new. I bet between his two boats he had over $150,000.00 investment. Even his deckhand was wearing one of those $400.00 camo coats. "Man, you're doing great then."

"It's just another payment." He held his arms to his chest, and continued hopping. There was something theatrical about this captain as he advised, "There are storm warnings out, seven foot waves on Douglas Channel. I suggest you take shelter in Collins Bay."

"Seven foot waves?"

"Yes, it'll sink your boat for sure." He pointed. "Collins Bay is up here on the right."

"Is that the one with the hot spring?"

"Yes, you can stay overnight there." He raised his hands high to illustrate. "Those waves are seven feet."

I nodded, continued to fill my tank, thinking it odd how he was painting the stormy picture, wondering if he might be staying there overnight as well, maybe looking for more hints on where that plane was because I've never seen any seven foot waves on Douglas Channel. But there wasn't a chance I'd stay at Collins Bay, I knew Jimmy was waiting.

The older deck hand hadn't said a word, just stared at me as if I were some kind of novelty.

The captain wasn't shy. "There's an average of twelve planes a year found around here."

I gave him a look, considering what a small world this was with satellite imagery and helicopters making short work of the back country.

At last I finished filling the 2nd tank and handed the empty to the deckhand. While he took it away, the captain replaced him, stepping to the side to hold onto my boat.

I cheerfully pulled my wallet out, righting myself, ready to hand the entire thing over to him if he wanted it. "What do I owe you?"

"This one's on me." He pushed the boat off, his palms springing open.

I was stunned at his generosity. For a second I was speechless, darn near breathless. At last I found my voice, "May God bless you."

Our two boats drifted apart and the captain disappeared inside the wheelhouse, leaving the deckhand staring across at me.

I was so taken with their kindness that my eyes watered. Again, I called out, "May God bless you!"

HOME AGAIN

They headed for Kemano and I headed for Kitimat. For the next ten miles there was no sign of the storm that the captain was talking about, but I hadn't hit Douglas Channel which is laid out east and west not north and south like Gardner.

After powering past Collins Bay, the boat started to hit some chop on the outskirts of Douglas. Looking ahead, I saw another boat in the distance. It was speeding for Kitimat. I joined the race to out distance the storm.

There was a definite chop on Douglas but nothing over three feet. Ahead, a Coast Guard pontoon boat was towing another boat in. The Coast Guard vessel must've had a powerful engine because there were a number of people onboard. A number of other boats were heading back to port, too. Perhaps they'd gotten the storm warning.

It was raining hard when I pulled into MK marina. I tied off and hurried down the planking, heading for the parking lot, wondering if Jimmy was there or in town. Gaining the parking lot, I grinned when I saw his Denali.

He had just laid down for his afternoon snooze when I popped my head up to his window. "Hey, Jimmy. How's it going?"

He looked like he wasn't sure if he were seeing a ghost. Finally he mumbled, "I've been worried about you."

It was still raining. I was soaking and wet by the time we pulled the boat out of the water.

When we got underway, Jimmy was in some hurry to get back to the States. I couldn't ask for a fellow who has more drive than he does. It didn't matter how rainy it was, or curvy the roads were, he just gets after it.

At that time I didn't tell him the dream I'd had in Kemano.

That entire trip was like a whirlwind. Jimmy wanted to drive straight back to the States, nonstop, and I supposed he would have, had some small town gas stations been open at night.

We got back the following evening. It was such a change to come back into our dry, smoke-filled land. The fire season had been bad.

My wife, Elaine, was quite surprised to see us back so soon. Jimmy, ever born under a wandering star, didn't even stay the night but was off again for Nevada. He certainly didn't let grass grow under his feet.

I will ever be grateful to Jimmy and his generosity in trading that boat for my camo truck. Additionally, he paid for most of the trip. May God bless you, Jimmy.

DREAM'S INTERPRETATION

I want to point out some disappointments that, to this day, bother me. Three times in my life the Lord clearly told me to witness to someone and I didn't. Each time, a month later that person died. The fact that they perished that shortly after was uncanny, so much so, that I felt like I had the Ghost Rider shadowing me. And why wasn't I obedient? I can only surmise a shallow relationship with my Maker. So, who am I to even deliver this message or have this dream?

I realize how severe the dream's interpretation is, but I don't want any more blood on my hands and I'm not here to sugarcoat it.

Before the sun set, I related the dream to Elaine, "Both black and white cannons were the same size, massive, half the size of the mountain. The white cannon was on the right, north side, same side as the downed plane. Black was on the south side. Both their guns were facing East, aimed directly at Kemano's power plant."

Her interpretation of it was precise. She started with Chief Mathews Bay. "One meaning of the word chief is source of origin. Mathew means – Gift of Yahweh."

This made sense because when I awoke from the dream, I felt like I'd been given a gift, as if that was the real reason I'd come.

"Because it was a dark night in your dream that means dark times are coming. From the size of the cannons, the phrase that comes to mind is, 'The shot that was heard around the world.'"

We looked up the phrase, 'The shot that was heard around the world.' Ralph Emerson penned it in the opening stanza of his Concord Hymn. It refers to the first shots fired in the American Revolutionary War. Since then, the phrase has been used in other events, including the assassination of Archduke Ferdinand of Austrian that sparked WW1.

"I figure because the cannons were aimed at Kemano, an electrical plant, the war that is coming is going to affect the power grid. An EMP?"

"Your trip doesn't make any sense to our natural man. The material man expects you to go out there and find a plane full of gold. But to God it makes perfect sense. Spiritually, the plane was tool to show you about things to come. Get back and write about things to come."

"Another intriguing point about the black and white cannons, they were right next to each other like a set of scales. The verse that comes to mind was the one Churchill used after Chamberlain signed the Munich Agreement in a vain attempt to prevent further expansion of the Nazis. 'Thou art weighed in the balances and found wanting.' Perhaps that's the word to North America. What's ironic about all this is how determined God is in warning us. When I consider the Kemano Power Plant, of all the power plants in North America, it should be the safest, most protected. What other power plant is built 1400 feet into a rock mountain? There really isn't a way the average citizen could drive to it. Even if they came in by boat and ended up at the dock, you still have to go another 10 miles to the plant. As far as access by plane the weather is always so foul

that even if there were some weird James Bond, comman-
do-style takeover, they'd have to wait forever for the skies
to clear."

At the end of the dream I saw what has become the cover
of this book, Warning, with the map of North America and
a view of a red reflective symbol and a peculiar snake in the
middle. It turned out to be Emergency Medical Services,
EMS, Star of Life symbol. The snake is wrapped around
a rod and there are a few accounts of this in the Bible,
Numbers 21:4-9 and John 3:14-15.

FATE

Finding the plane crash on the internet was like seeing the hand of Providence, hard to refute. That event truly tells me God is the Master Storyteller. Though it took 32 years to unfold, there was no doubt that I was handed a gift. Now I had to return to Chief Mathews Bay. I wanted to get that plane mystery completely solved.

When October 27, 2017 arrived, I looked at the weather report for Kitimat with the thought of going back before the snow flew. I had until Tuesday, October 31, before the forecast called for daytime temperatures to drop to 36 F. After November 1, daytime temperatures average 34 F, while at night it would be in the twenties with chances of snow.

Having jackknifed a boat on icy roads years before, I didn't desire to revisit that. Old man winter was coming. I could see that window was closing on a possible 2017 trip.

After meeting the mountain in Chief Mathews Bay, I figured God had better plans for me than being in such a hurry. Maybe that plane was no different to Him than an old car wreck. I sensed my priorities should be spent on getting this Dream Warning out before the events unfolded.

WOULD GOD BE BEHIND
THIS COMING WAR?

There are two trains of thought here. One – I don't see my God doing 9/11. That terrorist action was from Moslem terrorists, the pit of hell. But when a nation doesn't want God's ways, He backs away and takes His hand of protection with Him. Strange that people would blame Him for such an act when He's backed away.

The second train of thought is His judgment on a land. When a culture is anti-God, calling evil good and good evil, then it is ripe for judgment. This is like a father trying to shake up a son, snap him out of the direction he's going. Though there is a lot of pain going through it, it is the love of the Father that sends it. Rest assured, God won't be mocked. This nation will reap what it has sown, and perilous times will come.

The Bible tells us during Noah's time, God was so grieved of the wickedness of mankind that He decided to flood the earth. Another time of judgement is when he destroyed the towns of Sodom and Gomorra with fire and brimstone for their wickedness. And He had it in for Nineveh before they repented. And because Israel didn't keep His commandments and had turned to idols, He sent the Babylonians against them. Israel ended up as slaves in

Babylon for seventy years. Before each event, God gave them warnings.

Some say, "Because society has turned into a feely, feely, idol worshiping, thieving, adulterous, slandering, murdering thing, that God's judgment is coming."

Others say, "That's not the case, God's not out there to hammer on us, we simply reap what we have sown."

Commentators talk about economic waves and war cycles and how the current timing coincides with the *big one,* but there is little talk about God's judgment or God's principles of reaping and sowing.

How big will this war be?

I asked the Lord that question and a dream followed on November 17, 2017. I saw words written out on a piece of white paper but I didn't fully catch the first part of it. . . . *19% and another 10%*. I didn't understand the 10% part of it. I told the Lord this and had an immediate view of that Emergency Medical Symbol, EMS, the same one that ended the dream in Kemano. To my understanding, 19% will die due to the power outages, lack of food and water and 10% will die due to lack of emergency medical.

These numbers were so huge, over 100 million people, that I again asked my Lord if that was it?

Another dream followed – I was on a trek, going through a shadowy forest area around dusk, firmly holding three snakes. Two were in one hand with one in the other. One was a long skinny black thing. Another was a short fat snake with a diamond head. I don't recall the features of the third, perhaps it was so common that it didn't stand out. All were squirming, trying to get away but I held them firmly by their necks. What was odd, as we walked through this forest I saw someone looking over a woman's leopard skin satiny teddy, a satiny black bra and some other fancy clothes that were lying on the ground, and I wondered why anyone would take them in this time of struggle. Could one of these snakes think it was sexy?

Other people were with me but not a whole lot. I came to a steeper area where I needed my hands to shuffle down the landscape because the soil was glistening with clear oil atop it. So I tossed the snakes forward before I descended. They disappeared into the oily slippery slope. Strange that they could do that because it was small rock and dirt, not larger rock with crevices, yet it obviously had some quicksand features to it. I managed to avoid the oily surface, skirting around it.

At the bottom of the slope I found the fat snake just emerging from the oily surface and I snatched him as well as the long skinny black one. Both were squirming and covered with the oily muck. I firmly held them and looked for the third. There was something about time here, or the lack thereof, perhaps the sun was waning but I knew I couldn't be searching for the last snake forever, other people were gathering, waiting. I concluded that the last snake had died and we carried on. That was the end of the dream.

I asked the Lord for an interpretation and the understanding I got was that the snakes represent the US population and one of the snakes had perished = one third. Again, this was so bothersome that over a 100 million fellow Americans would perish that I hoped my interpretation was wrong. I prayed that this would not come to pass and I didn't care if I was even found out as some false interpreter, dreamer, whatever.

I again asked the Lord, "Are you sure that's the warning You want published?"

At the time of that prayer I was walking through our county government buildings looking for a meeting place regarding our tourism taxes. Within an hour of my question to the Lord, I encountered a gal that I hadn't seen in nearly a year. Raela was her name. It was a quick hello and goodbye because she was delivering mail for her job. She was part of our preparedness group, and, after she passed, the Lord reminded me that I'd used her name, Raela, in one of my books. He also reminded me that her character in said book had died, and that's what happens to people in a time of struggle.

Still I was disturbed by so many people perishing; the paradigm shift was just too great, so I asked again, "Are You really talking about a third of the population?"

That evening I watched a TV interview with Dr. Peter Vincent Pry, who has been the Executive Director of the task force on National Homeland Security, The Director of the US Nuclear Strategy Forum, and the Executive Director of the EMP task force on Homeland Security. Their commission is to look at weapons of mass destruction and cyber threats and make recommendations.

I was surprised that he believed N. Korea was capable of detonating a nuclear bomb over the US right now.

He pointed out that our vulnerability is great because of reliance on modern day electronics. If the nuclear blast happened above the atmosphere, 300-400 km high, the electric magnetic pulse, EMP, from it would knock out electronics in all 48 states. This intense energy would pass right through humans, not affecting them, but would have a killing effect on anything electronic. Nothing would work; you couldn't ship food or process it. If you were in an airline you'd be unable to fly. The devastation would be so severe it would send America back to the dark ages.

He said, "In the long run, we estimated that a nationwide blackout resulting from and EMP that could last a year could kill up to 90% of our population from starvation, disease . . ."

He also pointed out that DC runs in denial of this threat, the swamp doesn't get it, doesn't want to get it. I was also surprised to hear him say, "If congress had spent the money to harden the grid, back in 2010, then an EMP attack would be more manageable."

He went on to talk about cyber attacks rendering armies obsolete, and if an attacker took down the grid the game would be over.

Dr Pry saw Kim Jong-Un as a psychopath, who, besides being good at cheating on agreements, was a threat to humanity, and now was fully capable of hitting us.

Interestingly, he was an advocate of a preemptive strike on North Korea, explaining, "If they hit us first, there will be no coming back from an EMP attack."

After watching his interview I sat for a while, trying to digest it. His message was terribly sobering - it all made sense why so many of my dreams were with a dark background, no lights. What happened to the lights? I realized that my interpretation of one third the population perishing was far less than his 90% of the population. He went on to say it would be far worse than what the a-bomb did to Hiroshima, because it could wipe out a whole civilization.

I shouldn't have been surprised when he said, "DC wants to classify the reports so nobody outside the government can read about it."

Last year North Korea stated, "We will continue in preparing *preemptive* attacks with nuclear force."

I want to stop right here and ask you, the reader, if you'd pray that this message, this *warning* would get out. I feel a heavy burden that this nation is flying blind in a hellacious snow storm and our grid will crash, and I truly want to advise my fellow Americans to get ready. Pray that the masses will get a hold of this message like they did in Nineveh and repent, turning away from evil. Perhaps God will intervene yet.

NOTES

Jim Baker Show 2017, show#3375, Dec. 7, 2017

CYBER ATTACK

These days, when you think of cyber attacks it generally involves credit card and identity theft.

During George W. Bush's presidency, US and Israeli computer specialists launched a cyber attack on Iran's nuclear program. By introducing a computer worm, Stuxnet, they changed the speed of centrifuges, though the readings in the control room displayed, "normal." This disrupted the uranium refinement to the point that the centrifuges started to tear themselves apart. In the end it destroyed roughly a fifth of Iran's nuclear centrifuges, setting back their program by two years.

Imagine the same sort of cyber attack on our grid with inaccurate information flowing yet the, "Everything's fine," message displayed in the control room. In the meantime transformers are overloaded beyond their capacity with copper melting.

Our grid has over 3,000 companies that make it up. The problem is that they are all tied together. CEOs to some of the larger electrical companies believe that Russian and Chinese hackers are already inside our grid.

Having had two wind generators burn out, I know a little bit about the power of electricity. The problem with wind generators is that they have an exponential factor. Higher speeds don't just double the amp output but increase it by a factor of 10 or more. And there is no slowing down those blades once they get really rolling without damaging the braking mechanism. If you can't get rid of that power fast enough, then copper heats up and burns out. This is no different than the US grid. Power is constantly flowing in from power plants, and that power has to be gobbled up or the system goes beyond its capacity. Once the transformers max out then something burns.

If hackers are able to take down one of the large power transformers, LPT, there would be a cascading effect, burning out more transformers. The cost of one of these LPT are up to 10 million, each is individually designed, mostly made overseas and take up to two years to replace. Spares, what spare? Weighing up to 600,000 lbs, these aren't easily moved, so just to get them down the road or on a railcar is a feat. Bottom line, if these transformers are smoked, power returning quickly isn't going to happen.

George Cotter, a former chief scientist at the National Security Agency, authored a white paper in April 2015, – *Security in the North America Grid – A Nation at Risk.* He concludes: "Incredibly weak cyber security standards with a wide open communications and network fabric virtually guarantees success to major nation-states and competent hacktivists. This industry is simply unrealistic in believing in the resiliency of this grid subject to a sophisticated attack. When such an attack occurs, make no mistake, there will be major loss of life and serious crippling of National Security capabilities."

Former secretaries of defense, Ashton Carter and Leon Panetta, indirectly and directly, express similar worries.

Notes

"The Stuxnet Attack On Iran's Nuclear Plant Was 'Far More Dangerous' Than Previously Thought". Business Insider. 20 November 2013

Panetta warned that an aggressor nation or extremist group: Transcript, U. S. Department of Defense, October 11, 2012.

Aston Carter indirectly express similar worries: US Department of Department of Defense, DOD Cyber Strategy, April 2015

Commando attack

On April 16, 2013 a commando style attack took out the PG & E Company's Metcalf Transmission Substation in California. It took 27 days to bring the substation back.

After doing a study of the attack, Jon Wellinghoff, chairman of the Federal Energy Regulatory Commission, FERC, thinks this was a trial run for a bigger attack.

It's not hard to imagine a concerted commando attack on the main substations throughout the country. If nine of the country's main substations were knocked out simultaneously, FERC analysis conclude it would blackout most of the US grid.

I find this case the most intriguing of them all. Some say this could be instigated by independent actors such as ISIS. But what if it was done by a close knit group of Americans? To think that it could be done by a team, not from outside the country, but inside the country, is frightening. Would that be the beginnings of a civil war?

If that was the case, fake news can send the blame anywhere.

We used to be a nation who'd recite the Pledge of Allegiance in schools on a daily basis; a nation that, even with a two party system, would be able to cross the aisle and work together on legislation. Part of that Pledge was the word *Indivisible.* Question – are we undivided any longer? Or are we so divided that opposition will do whatever it takes to slander a President's appointed Supreme Court justice before a vote?

They say, *all is fair in love and war* but if that commando attack on PG & E Transmission Substation is a trial run for a bigger attack then lookout.

NOTES

"Assault on California Power Station Raises Alarm on Potential for Terrorism," Rebecca Smith, *Wall Street Journal*, February 5, 2014

EMP ATTACK

In *Electromagnetic Pulse Protection* article, Jerry Emanuelson, B.S.E.E., Futurescience, says, "The threat of a sudden EMP attack that causes a widespread catastrophe is certainly an old problem. Consider this Cold War era quotation from a widely-read and highly-respected publication more than 35 years ago: "The United States is frequently crossed by picture-taking Cosmos series satellites that orbit at a height of 200 to 450 kilometers above the earth. Just one of these satellites, carrying a few pounds of enriched plutonium instead of a camera, might touch of instant coast-to-coast pandemonium: the U.S. power grid going out, all electrical appliances without a separate power supply (televisions, radios, computers, traffic lights) shutting down, commercial telephone lines going dead, special military channels barely working or quickly going silent." – from "Nuclear Pulse (III): Playing a Wild Card" by William J. Broad in **Science** magazine, pages 1248-1251, June 12, 1981.

As a whole, because our government and people are a reactive society not a preventative one, we will take the bullet first and try to put Humpty Dumpty back together afterward. This is doomed to fail. Experts say, if an EMP hits, the geomagnetic wave could destroy the largest transformers on the power grid, effectively shutting it down.

So without electricity to pump or make fuel, how do service vehicles get down the road to start putting Humpty Dumpty back together? The turning point of such an event would be so radical, such a great shock, that it would very quickly turn into a meat grinder.

Our government has no plan in place for such a large event. Previously there were plans to harden the grid against an EMP attack but it didn't get beyond the Senate.

Though first responders and FEMA did a great job on hurricane Sandy, they will have a difficult time getting to work. Even if they got to work, what would their work place look like without the use of phones, working toilets, electricity?

Additionally, why is it the first responsibility of government to somehow get everything back together when our first priority should be to look after our own families' and neighbors' basic needs?

NOTES:

Electromagnetic Pulse Protection, Jerry Emanuelson, 2009-2017

"Nuclear Pulse (III): Playing a Wild Card" by William J. Broad in Science magazine, pages 1248-1251, June 12, 1981.

War from the Heavens

With one cannon being black and the other white this may be a war that God has set against us. If it is, perhaps He's warning us that a solar storm has been called up to attack our grid.

In 1859 a geomagnetic solar storm called the Carrington Event hit the earth. They're caused by coronal mass ejections, eruptions on the sun. It was one of the largest geomagnetic storms on record. Auroras were seen around the world. Telegraph systems failed, in some cases giving telegraph operators electric shocks.

In 1989, a similar solar storm shut down the power grin in Quebec, causing over 19 billion in damages. Two transformers were damaged due to voltage overloads.

Based on historical aurora records, estimate return period of a Carrington-level is 150 years, ranging between 100-250 years.

In 2013, a Lloyd's of London and Atmospheric and Environmental Research in the U.S., estimated if a similar event happened today it would cost between $.6-2.6 trillion, and possibly shut the grid down in certain areas for up to two years. They estimated millions of people would be directly affected by this.

NOTES:

Philips, Tony (January 21, 2009). "Severe Space Weather-Space and Economic Impacts". NASA Science: Science News. science.nasa.gov

Committee on the Societal and Economic Impacts of Severe Space Weather Events: A Workshop, National Research Council (2008) . Severe Space Weather Events-Understanding Societal and Economic Impacts: A Workshop Report, National Academies Press. P.13.

"Solar storm risk to north American electric grid" (PDF)

WHAT NATION CAN DISRUPT OUR GRID?

IRAN

Some say Iran is the most aggressive player in the Middle East. It relentlessly fans the fires of sectarian hatred with its support of Assad in Syria, Hamas in Israel, Hezbollah in Lebanon, and the Houthis in Yemen. Estimates of their annual support of Assad vary, but it is in the billions. Religious war is so important to them that they have sacrificed their own economy to support those groups.

In 2017 Turkey, Russia, and Iran came together with talks regarding Syria. It was an unusual combination because Turkey is a Nato ally. It wasn't that long ago that they shot down a Russian jet.

Interestingly, Ezekiel 38 predicts a big attack on Israel in the latter days and theologians believe that three of the main players in said prophesy are Turkey, Russia and Iran. Also interesting, it is the first time in history that all three armies are in Syria. Syria just happens to border Israel.

With Iran's aggression, a direct war has grown likely between them and Israel.

The US is also in Syria, supporting the Kurds, with or without the blessing of Assad.

Presently Turkey is pushing into Syria in their fight against the Kurds.

For Iran to have a successful attack on Israel, their war planners know the US has to go. They have missiles but we believe none can hit our continent. That might not be true because they are a stealth operator that has cooperated with Russia and North Korea for a long time.

Iran is no little boy when it comes to warfare. On December 4, 2011, they brought down a US drone, RQ-170, successfully capturing it. That was no small feat, considering the decoding and cyber work involved to land it safely. And that was 7 years ago. Presently they are claiming to have a secret weapon that can sink our ships.

Matthew 24:6 speaks of the last days, wars and rumors of war.

CHINA

The 21st century appears to be China's. The sun will rise and shine on the dragon. They now have the fastest computers and an economy driven by 1.4 billion consumers and more billionaires than the US. They are zooming into the future on their high speed trains, planes, autonomous buses, LED lights, smart phones and TVs, to cutting edge facial recognition for their entire population. And lately they've been buying up companies around the world.

Part of the problem with all their growth is they need

oil and they're aggressively going after it, building islands in controversial waters to protect shipping lanes. Their leadership likes to wine and dine our leadership and has a 275 billion trade surplus with the US. When push comes to shove, however, China generally sides with our enemies. Last year they had naval drills with Iran. Lately, they launched the DF-17, a ballistic missile that flies at low altitudes, too low for detection.

Our military has identified China as one of the main players in cyber attacks.

According to Bill Gertz from The Washington Free Beacon, "China is building an array of high technology space arms, anti-satellite missiles, lasers, GPS jammers and killer satellites that Beijing says will give its military strategic advantage in a future conflict with the United States."

NOTES

Asia Now Has More Billionaires Than the U.S., Katya Kazakina and Patrick Winters, Bloomberg, Oct. 25, 2017

China's Great Leap in space warfare creates huge new threat, Bill Gertz, 14 September 2017

RUSSIA

When Trump won the presidency, opposition was so infuriated that they blamed the entire election on the Russians, "those evil Russians."

Since Russia's invasion of Crimea in 2014, they have been penalized by a number of sanctions from the US and

EU which have hampered their economy, caused a flight of capital and devalued the Ruble. With low oil prices they are barely staying out of a recession. It's unfortunate for the average Russian suffering under rising costs from the sanctions.

If you read NATO Review, any mention of Russia generally has the word *evil* as they pound the drums against the bear from the north.

What I find perplexing is why Russia is always painted with a dark brush. I think we can agree that ISIS was the biggest evil in the last 3 years, not Russia. Didn't Russia do a decent job against ISIS in Syria? Bizarre that the US, who helped create ISIS, is putting sanctions on Russia.

The American press always paints the picture of *evil* Putin, continually poking at him. I'm sure he's not perfect but which one of our presidents was perfect?

Sometimes I wonder if this dark painting of Russia isn't inspired by America's war machine and the Pentagon's need for a bad guy to somehow justify their 660 billion dollar budget.

In 2016 NATO took another poke at the Russians with its deployment of ballistic missiles in Romania.

Last year, the US sent 1,000 men, 87 tanks and 144 armoured vehicles to Poland and plans to ratchet up their force there to 4,000. Poland is happy to have them as long as we shoulder the cost.

As of March 1, 2018 the US announced the sale of anti-tank missiles to Ukraine over Russian opposition.

Russian deputy foreign minister, Sergei Ryabkov, responded, "The United States in a certain sense crossed the line . . ."

Pray there's not a day when the bear gets cornered

because Russia has some tools in its military box that might surprise the west.

Of late, Putin announced a new nuclear missile that travels at over 4,000 mph, cannot be intercepted and can strike anywhere in the world. When touting this invincible weapon, Putin came across with attitude, near angry, implying they will use it if provoked, "No matter what the consequences are."

He got a standing ovation from his government officials.

Who knows if he was bluffing about this futuristic weapon, but we didn't appreciate Russian missiles in Cuba when Kennedy was President, so why would they appreciate our destroyers, powering though the Black Sea, loaded with the hot stuff?

Notes

U.S. launches long-awaited European missile defense shield, CNN, May 12, 2016

Russia says US troops arriving in Poland pose threat to its security, Ewen MacAskill, The Gaurdian, 12 Jan. 2017

US will provide anti-tank weapons to Ukraine, State Dept. official says, CNN WIRE, Dec. 23, 2017

North Korea

Since Kim Jong Un took leadership of North Korea in 2011, he has executed 340 people, including his uncle and half brother. Seventy high ranking officers were part of this cleanse, cementing his reign of terror.

Amnesty International estimates 120,000 people wallow away in prison camps, subject to systematic, widespread and gross human rights violations.

Soldiers who have escaped say that food is scarce. South Korean doctors found tapeworms as long as 27cm. in one soldier wounded during a daring escape.

The regime has a history of lack of compassion for its citizens. In the 1990's some estimate around 3 million starved to death during a famine. Famine continues today. Due to malnutrition and starvation, North Korean preschool children average 1.2 to 1.6 inches shorter than S. Koreans.

UN sanctions aren't helping this dire situation. North Korea remains relentless in its pursuit of nuclear weapons and, with the help of rogue nations, has been able to navigate into some world trade. Though, food and oil are its Achilles heel.

With Trump's calling out any nations that are trading with North Korea, it appears the screws are being tightened.

A recent article from North Korean state run newspaper has advised its citizens, "We will have to chew the roots of plants once again."

Even though a preemptive strike would be suicide for them, with new sanctions, and our president calling a spade a spade, this may turn into a Jim Jones, self fulfilling prophesy. But before they drink the purple drink, Kim Jong Un may initiate the war, pushing the button, launching the weapon. His people are starving and he's cornered, isolated, not logical, delusionary and threatened. With nuclear weapons at his disposal, that's a bad combination.

Thank God Trump has initiated some peace talks with Kim Jong Un. But this is a nation that has broken lots of treaties.

NOTES

North Korea Executions under Kim Jong Un, George Petras, USA Today, Feb. 10, 2016

North Korea 2017/2018 www.amnestry.org

Are North Koreans really three inches shorter than South Koreans?, Richard Knight, BBC News, 23 April 2012

North Korea Tells Citizens to Prepare Themselves for Famine, Nash Jenkins, Time, March 29, 2016

A PEACEFUL SOLUTION?

We have a friend who sells real-estate out in Herlong, California. Herlong is approximately 50 miles north of Reno, on the map because of an Army base.

She didn't know I was writing this *Warning* and last mouth I got in touch with her. "How's it going with the Army base, are they staying busy or will they be shutting down?"

"We are going to war."

"Really?"

"The base is busier than ever. They're hiring. Yes, they are gearing up for war."

"How can you be so sure?"

"Trains are coming in and going out, one after another. They're also rehiring retired military, bringing them back for this one. We're going to war."

It will be interesting to see how this meeting with Trump and Kim Jong Un goes. But Kim's not the only gun in town; with the US selling tank killers to Ukraine, and pressing our missiles closer to the Russian border, Putin's not happy with us. Also early rounds of a trade war are developing with China. Trade wars generally don't end well, more often ending in real wars. China also wants Taiwan back. Lately, their prime minster, Xi Jinping, added, ". . . resolved to fight the bloody battle against our enemies."

Jesus declares in Mathew, 24:7, "For nation will rise against nation, and kingdom against kingdom. And there will be famines, pestilences, and earthquakes in various places."

Who's to say, this nation won't be attacked by a number of nations.

We need to pray that this country repents, and pray for peace.

NOTES

China ready to fight 'bloody battle' against enemies, Xi says in speech, James Griffiths, CNN, March 20, 2018

Signs of the Times

I'm not the only one crying out in the wilderness, sounding the alarm. The Doomsday Clock put out by Science and Security Board says we are at 2 ½ minutes to chaos, and they are a secular board. Some events happen fast, some slow, but since the 1970's they say that 58% of all worldwide wildlife is gone, and 50% of coral is gone. Since 1950 when they started to record climate-related disasters, 30 per year then, now we have 300-400 a year. In the last year alone there have been five 1000 year floods in the US.

Major earthquakes are becoming more common. Areas that don't normally get earthquakes are getting them. Presently, Yellowstone is trembling with thousands of quakes. We are seeing bigger hurricanes; 2017 was the only season on record that three hurricanes had accumulated cyclone energy of over 40.

Christ speaks of the signs of the times in Matt. 16:2-3; the world is shifting, moaning for His return.

Worldwide, there have been massive forest fires. As of August, 2017, in the US there were 1.8 million acres burned above the ten year average. The costliest year for fires, freezing, floods and hurricanes was 2017, coming in at $306 billion. In Europe, the total was roughly three times the normal amount of summer fires. The start of 2018 has turned into another record breaker for weather – southern

California had the hottest January ever recorded and Moscow had the most snow on record.

Worldwide, hatred of Christians has dramatically accelerated. In the Middle East, hundreds of thousands of Christians have been persecuted and martyred, to the point that it is called, "Genocide". The increase in Christian persecution incidents in India has never been so great.

Our nation is at an interesting time in history; since we gave up traditional values our gold has flowed eastward toward Asia at an unprecedented rate. Real money is leaving. Perhaps that's another sign that our time in the sun has passed. Imagine what would happen if people lost faith in the mighty greenback.

We're also seeing signs of greater division in this country between liberals and conservatives. It is nothing new to hear opposition talking of killing elected officials.

Daily, law enforcement struggles to keep society in check. Police are regularly getting shot, more and more in ambush shootings, and, when they shoot back, their lives go under a microscope. Monthly, there are school shootings.

We can also see a dying church, the falling away, people who are easily offended, a generation that has spent countless hours idol worshiping at their computers, downloading sexual experiences, worshiping humanism, and glamorizing homosexuality. We also see how paganism is taking hold in the US. Last year, the Burning Man had over 70,000 attendees.

We can also see the falsity of the media. Just the other day the stock market went up 300 points only to drop nearly the same after an erroneous report on ABC News. During the latest presidential elections a former CNN commentator relayed questions ahead of the debate to Hillary Clinton. Since Trump has been elected the news is relentless on the Russians who supposedly hacked the election. What news can you trust?

NOTES

The 2017 fire season is a global phenomenon. Kendra Pierre-Louis, Popular Science, August 4, 2017

Indian Christians faced almost as many attacks in first half of 2017 as all of 2016, World Watch Monitor, August 8, 2017

William J. Broad in Science magazine, pages 1248-1251, June 12, 1981.

Trump suggest investors sue ABC reporter whose erroneous report sent stocks down, Kyle Feldscher, Washington Examiner, Dec. 03, 2017

Donna Brazile finally admits she shared debate questions with Clinton campaign, Eddie Scarry, Washington Examiner, March 17, 2017

Wars the United States has been involved in the last 50 years.

Vietnam – 2,000,0000 casualties, 25-year war. I say 25-year war because we weren't just drawn in by President Kennedy in the early 60's but shouldered 80% of the French costs during the 1950's. The French were responsible for over 1,000,000 Vietnamese deaths.

Seven million tons of bombs were dropped on Vietnamese, triple what we used in all off WWII. Some of those unexploded bombs are still going off today, killing and maiming farmers, rendering their agriculture useless. Eleven million gallons of toxic chemicals also rendered their soil useless. In Cambodia, US pilots literally dropped bombs on lakes, over and over again.

Casualty numbers in Laos and Cambodia are more difficult to assess as those were secret wars.

Iraq – casualty estimates vary from 150,000 to 460,000.

Afghanistan – casualties aren't yet totaled, after 16 years that war is still ongoing. It's called, Operation Enduring **Freedom**.

The Libya war has dragged on into its eighth year. Libya used to be a country that had stability. Not since our bombs hit them.

And presently, the same is played out in Yemen as the US supports Saudi Arabia's ambitions there. Since Yemen's health system has been shattered they've had the largest Cholera outbreak ever recorded. This is a country of 27 million and 16 million have no water.

It appears the US destabilized the Middle East, having a hand in creating ISIS. Millions of poor people were displaced in one of the largest exodus ever recorded. Christians took the brunt of the attacks; death and starvation followed.

What were the casualties of US soldiers in those oversea wars? Countless, as casualties never measure the drug and alcohol additions in the aftermath, let alone widows, fatherless families, family breakups, PTS and suicide.

Through it all, some say no other nation has pushed the world toward the End Times more than the United States of America.

NOTES

Charles Hirschman et al., "Vietnam Casualties During the American War: The New Estimate." Population and Development Review, December 1995.

80 percent of the cost of war, Zinn, A People's History of the United States. P.471 toxic chemicals, "pellow-2007-159"

Wright, Rebecca (2016-0906). "'My friends were afraid of me': What 80 million unexploded US bombs did to Laos". CNN Retrieved 2016-09-18

"Yemen cholera epidemic reaches 'devastating proportions' as deaths mount". ABC News Australia. 11 June 2017

THIS COMING WAR

With unemployment low, construction robust, and bellies full, people have no worries of ill times ahead. Despite our government debt, everything seems stable now.

Was it any different before 9/11? Was it any different during the time of Noah?

Presently, Americans don't have an appetite to get into a ground war with North Korea or Iran but that could change on a dime if our grid was knocked down. Even if it were knocked out by a cyber attack, if Washington DC could pin it on Iran or North Korea, like they somehow pinned 9/11 on Saddam Hussein, or as they pinned the sinking of the Maine on the Spanish, drawing us into the Spanish-American war, or as they pinned the phony Bay of Tonkin incident on North Vietnam, then look out, we'll go to war.

If this war is against North Korea, and China gets rubbed the wrong way and puts boots on the ground against us then WWIII is on.

It is one thing to experience war's domino effect when technology is slow, it will be quite another to experience it when targets are already locked in, GPS positioned, and all Navy sailors have to do is push the button. War planners will wake up the following morning and be amazed at what's transpired. Rest assured, this won't be our father's war where the firing goes in all directions but a war that is fought with big bombs and high speed missiles that go straight down smoke stacks as well as streaking through outer space, taking out military satellites.

The complications of this next war will quickly bring idealism and expectancy to their knees. The public will be on its toes to hear any shred of news from overseas. Rest assured fake news will abound.

If it is a war with N Korea, and South Korean casualties are involved, if you think the politicians are less than candid with the American people now, they will go into a shell then.

Interestingly, those cannons in that dream weren't gray and white but black and white which indicate that they will separate parties and people. Opposition to the war will be great. They are going to think us evil, and we are going to think them evil.

If this war happens under Trump's presidency, any wrong military decisions by him will be magnified by the American press. Those rogues will blame everything from earthquakes to the change in weather on him. If China and Russia get involved, become our adversary, and the sons and daughters of our nation end up at the bottom of the Chinese Sea, professors in this country will pick apart our president's very religion. They'll smear his reelection possibilities as laughable. But they won't say a word of God's cleansing judgment on a defiled land.

WHERE IS ISRAEL IN THIS WAR?

Over the years, Israel has leaned on the US for help, at least militarily. But when this forthcoming war knocks out the US electrical grid, our downfall will accelerate. Israel will become isolated. When their survival has to count only on God and God alone, then perhaps they'll truly find their Messiah.

The encouraging part of this is there are more and more Messianic Jews on the airwaves. Perhaps we're getting closer to the time where the 144,000 Jewish evangelicals will be unleashed.

WHEN WILL THIS WAR START?

Date wise, I will not make a prediction. It may happen sooner than expected but, with God slow to anger, He may be giving the nation a bit of a reprieve, a chance to repent.

Christ tells us in Matt. 24: 38-39 For as in the days before the flood, they were eating and drinking, marrying and giving in marriage, until the day that Noah entered the ark, and did not know until the flood came and took them all away, so also will the coming of the Son of Man be."

Here, it sounds like the economy will be rolling great before the flood comes. Interestingly, Noah preached for a good long time before God flooded the earth, yet in Jonah's time, Nineveh was only given forty days.

The reason I think it might happen sooner than later is how fast that trip to Kemano came about. Within a week of Jimmy's call (Saturday) we had purchased a boat in Idaho, driven it to Montana then 1250 miles to Kitimat, BC, where I cruised down the channel, into Kemano on that Friday night (six days). That night I had the – warning- dream.

Regardless, when the war starts, with those cannons in the dream being over 2000 feet tall, it indicates to me the event won't be subtle.

Once this war gets rolling, despite how bright the politicians, they could have their hands full with bad decisions.

It will be as if our nation has a predestined meeting with a sea monster that will take us into deeper, darker waters.

If this war comes to our shores in the form of an electro-magnetic pulse, then hell will step down on earth. Trust in society will evaporate. Civil unrest may escalate to civil war with a hard core takeover by one side.

It may be as if God has stepped off the planet. People will look for a comforting place, but they won't find one.

We can do a lot of *what ifs* here and, when we are dealing with nuclear, it becomes a very dangerous game, but *what if* we repent? The people of Nineveh repented and God changed their future. I pray this nation humbles itself, gets on its knees and gets right with God. I mean really repents, and quickly.

How will our government respond to a nationwide power outage that goes on and on?

Presently governments are readying for war, ramping up their military, bloating their budgets even more.

In the beginning there will be martial law. Military will do their best to keep order. When food runs low, livid citizens will be out to torch the White House and police will be besieged. When hunger rules, even the military won't be able to stop riots, looting and destruction. When goods dry up and emergency services break down, then look out.

Good luck to those who count on Social Security, food assistance, or anything from the government. The greatest mistake people will make is trusting in the sense of security that our government provides. Who's to say the higher-ups in government won't be in their own bunkers, weapons pointed outward, with no thought of sharing their food and water with the public.

Hordes will be out to get what they figure is theirs, one way or another.

A dark blanket will fall upon the unprepared public. Overwhelmed, the disillusioned will quickly fall by the wayside. Good luck to those who are traveling, who are going into uncertain areas.

When this occurs it will be like Rev 6:4, Another horse, fiery red, went out. And it was granted to the one who sat on it to take peace from the earth, and that people should kill one another; and there was given to him a great sword.

The government will be scrapping to survive just like everyone else. If you have something they need, they'll be coming. They might come under the halo of "community." If you have lots of food, you might be tagged a hoarder, a terrorist, extremist, or they may claim you stole it from some soup kitchen.

Rest assured, no man's goods or life will be safe.

HOW BAD WILL IT GET?

C hrist says in Rev: 22, 11 **"He who is unjust, let him be unjust still: he who is filthy, let him be filthy still; he who is righteous, let him be righteous still; he who is holy, let him be holy still."** This may seem like a strange comment because he almost encourages those who do evil to keep it up, stick a fork in it. But examining the verse, I believe what He's saying is He's not returning until there's real moral decay. Can't you see it happening in the falling away, sexual promiscuity, shallow preaching, senseless shootings, pervasive drug culture, lack of respect for parents, ongoing terrorism and an unaccountable government?

There will be a push back from the people of faith but it won't be enough to overcome what's coming. Look out when money dies, and the grid goes down.

WILL REVIVAL RETURN TO THIS LAND?

I t is encouraging to hear of Moslems coming to Christ and see the pictures of the millions in Africa who are submitting to Him. I know the Spirit is mysterious enough to move His hand upon our land and turn this ship around. Who knows if the Spirit will put unbiblical laws in this country back in the bottle or reduce that pervasive harlot in DC? Without another revolution, I think not.

Moreover, the Apostle Paul tells us in 2 Thes. 2:3 that a falling away comes first. And Revelation doesn't speak of any revivals either. Rev. 9: 20-21 But the rest of mankind, who were not killed by these plagues, did not repent of the works of their hands, that they should not worship demons, and idols of gold, silver, brass, stone, and wood, which can neither see nor hear nor walk. And they did not repent of their murders or their sorceries or their sexual immorality or their thefts.' Fascinatingly, here mankind sees the incredible events of Revelation yet still won't repent.

HOW DO WE PREPARE FOR WAR?

There are a lot of phases of war. In the dream of the cannons, both were pointed east, back toward Kemano's power plant. God help us if North America loses electricity for a long time. Matt. 24: 7 speaks of famines.

Proverbs 22:3 tells what a prudent man does when he foresees evil. 1 Timothy 5:8 says that we are worse than an infidel if we don't look after our own.

The coastal, metropolitan areas will be hit the hardest. The few that stockpile Mountain #10 cans, rice and beans, and have an off grid heat source and water will fare the best, but there may be laws deterring hoarding.

Presently, there are plenty of prep places to purchase food. Jim Baker.com puts out good products. Food is cheap now, but it won't be when the lights go out.

In the dream one canon was white and the other black. In Revelation the action for the Great Tribulation is kicked-off by the first horse, (Rev 6:2) a white horse and it went out to conquer; the black horse is the third horse (Rev 6:5,6) and its rider had a pair of scales in his hand. It brought famine.

Water is as important as food. If you have a well and you have the wherewithal to get a hand pump, then you're ahead of the game. When I was a kid in Concord, Ca, I was surprised to see that we had a well in the backyard. Who knows if it has dried up since, but this was right in the metropolis. A simple hand pump could supply life giving water if the power went down.

If you can't afford a well with a hand pump, then try to buddy up with someone who has one. Be sure to purchase a water purifier. If you are in the city, you might need to make some country connections. Be prepared to walk.

A wood stove for heating and cooking would be vital. Its ambiance is great on a cold winter evening.

When you prepare for disaster, keep in mind the importance of oil for cooking. The body must have oil to survive. Find oil that will go the distance. Stored at the right temperature, flax seeds are a long lasting source. Don't forget your vitamins. Vitamin C is very important, keeps rickets at bay.

I was surprised to learn that our government has tagged September as Prepared Month. I think they are indirectly saying, "There's a lot going on behind the scenes that you might want to get ready for."

Our government has a good website www.ready.gov/make-a-plan. It will give you good insight on what you need. Don't forget pet preparedness for your furry friends.

Electromagnetic Pulse Protection is an excellent article by Jerry Emanuelson, B.S.E.E., Futurescience, LLC. It is well worth reading.

Your neighbors will be crucial following a disaster. Getting to know them now builds trust. Seeing your neighbor on a daily basis doesn't always lead to knowing them on a personal level. Surely you'd rather work with them before an emergency than see them aim a weapon at you later. We must love our neighbor as our self. The entire law is summed up in – loving your neighbor as yourself. The Bible says two are better than one, so strength in numbers is good.

You may be reading this and say to yourself, "If my neighbor doesn't have any food, why should I reach out to them when I'm doing all the providing?"

Two trains of thought here: one could say, "That's part of the Christian walk. If we perish through those actions, God will balance the books." The other thought, "How can I provide for my family if I give all my food away to my hungry neighbors?"

It's true, if food runs low, people will be coming out of the woodwork, looking for handouts, on the prowl for yours (some individual's type of preparing is buying a gun and taking what you have). It won't just be your neighbor but also his brother across town, knocking on your door. Let's be frank: if you simply give your food away, you might get some temporary glory out of it, but your handout implies that you have lots. You will be targeted.

Who knows if this won't be the time where Christ mentions in Matt. 24:12 "And because lawlessness will abound, the love of many will grow cold."

Where's wisdom? Revelation tells us during that time, a quart of wheat will be traded for a day's wage. That means commerce will be tough, but still ongoing. Bottom line, don't just give it away, have them work for it, but always feign that you barely have enough to feed your family.

If you are able to come together as a neighborhood, then you should have security patrols and a plan, a safe meeting place, a first-aid attendant, and a communications specialist. Someone needs to be responsible to turn off gas lines. There should be a plan to look after seniors and the disabled. Hopefully people will help one another so it won't turn into The Little Red Hen scenario where people want to be fed without lifting a finger.

The problem with North Americans is that we are so independent and busy that we hardly notice a new resident, let alone have them over for dinner. In my neighborhood most interaction is done over keeping poachers out during hunting season, but what we need is a yearly potluck.

When I considered the dream and the size of those cannons – half the size of the mountain, I asked the Lord, "Will the U.S. win the war?" All I got back was the reminder of that florescent warning sign, Emergency Medical Services, EMS. With no access to Medical Services and prescription drugs, I imagine there will be no end of death.

Some say guns and bullets are important to keep the bad boys at bay as well as silver and gold coins to trade with, but the real answer isn't found in stuff but in a relationship with the Lord, Jesus. He will show you what you need to do, how you need to prepare.

Complacency is huge in this country. A lot of very successful people don't even have a week's supply of food and regard prepping as pure hillbilly. Preppers will not win a popularity contest with mainstream media, but that's good because silence is where you need to be in your prepping.

Explaining the End Times, Jesus says, Mt. 24:10 "And then many will be offended, will betray one another, and will hate one another."

Besides warning us, I think He's trying to tell us how important it is to be quiet and careful. It sounds like family members will rat you out and families will be torn apart. So you must prepare quietly, without anyone noticing. Try not to leave a paper trail with your purchases.

If this is the *big one* then our compassion for humanity will grow cold. Aggression will be the new format. When one wakes up in the morning, his prayer will be to make it through the day without getting shot as it will be difficult to tell friend from foe. Most importantly, regardless of how bad it gets, we need to be forgiving.

I don't want to live with a survivalist mentality because some of that wears on your happiness, but I want to be prepared. My grandfather's generation had the cultural values and knowledge of pioneer stock where they could live with or without electricity, but that isn't the case anymore. Imagine living on the 32nd floor of some high rise when the power goes out: elevators don't move, and the only water is in a dirty river, five miles away.

WHAT IF MY NEIGHBOR IS A WACKO DACO?

I f you think gun toting, tattooed Chucky is less honorable than straight forward George you might be surprised when chaos rules. It comes down to the heart. Who knows another man's heart?

Dialog is so important during times of struggle. The Bible tells us a soft answer will turn away wrath. Jesus tells us that during the End Times people will be easily offended. In the beginning I bet emotions will be running high. There'll be lots of drama. I plan on really watching my tongue.

There may be a wide variety of religious beliefs in your neighborhood. There is a wide range of beliefs in the preparedness group I attend. After sticking my foot in my mouth enough times to knock out my teeth, I stay away from things that separate, and, regardless of how different the person's beliefs are, I try to respectfully honor the individual and work on things we have in common. Rest assured, when the lights go out, everyone who contributes to the group's efforts in staying alive will be valued.

A NOTE TO THE AFFLUENT

I f God has given you the funds to make it happen, to prepare for the forthcoming storm, you shouldn't just prepare for yourself and yours but for your neighborhood. If electricity goes down for a long time, the affluent will need the protection of their neighbors because one of the first things the hungry do is target the rich. Your protection may depend on you truly looking after, and providing food for your neighbors. By yourself you cannot do a 24/7 security forever, but it's a different story if you have the help of your neighbors.

If you have the means to go this route, then do it with the right attitude. After Jesus was crucified, a rich man from Arimathea, Joseph, went to Pilate and asked for the body of Jesus. One version says, begged for the body of Jesus. What it shows is a determined man who ended up using myrrh and aloes, binding Christ's body with strips of linen and placing him in a new tomb in which no one had been laid. You can see it cost Joseph something, and he didn't do it second class.

In my first book, Everyone Left Behind, 4 minutes to chaos, the main character, Hershal, has a dream that is interpreted to store up for 70 people for a period of 5 years. Hershal's wife is a Christian and gung-ho to get started, but not Hershal. The cost was too great.

If you see this train coming and have the money to do something about it yet don't, then you shouldn't be surprised when the storm comes and you and your house are swept away.

You can checkout anytime

I n life, when things don't go the way one anticipates, a certain percent of the population simply checks out. It doesn't seem to matter if the person is affluent or poor, they both check out. Who knows if their brain is so overwhelmed with the situation that they slip into denial, or fantasy, and cover it with drugs, booze, entertainment, or idol worship? Was the *check out* caused by earlier addictions, temptations from the devil, or is it's simply a lazy form of living?

Then again, it could simply be their way of saying, "If I don't get it my way then I'm checking out."

This has a major impact on society, on marriages, families, work and politics. Alcoholism alone costs this country 249 billion dollars a year.

Fortunately God doesn't check out. Thank God!

Christ reminds us, John 16:33 "These things I have spoken to you, that in Me you may have peace. In the world you will have tribulation; but be of good cheer, I have overcome the world."

He challenges us to *overcome*. Rev. 2:7 "He that has an ear, let him hear what the Spirit says to the churches. To him who overcomes I will give to eat from the tree of life, which is in the midst of the Paradise of God." Rev. 2:26 "And he who overcomes, and keeps My works until the end, to him I will give power over the nations– Rev. 3:5 "He who overcomes shall be clothed in white garments, and I will not blot out his name from the Book of Life; but I will confess his name before My Father and before His angels. Rev. 3:21 "To him who overcomes I will grant to sit with Me on My throne, as I also overcame and sat down with My Father on His throne."

He also reminds us of what happens to those who don't overcome, Rev. 21: 7-8 "He who overcomes shall inherit all things, and I will be his God and he shall be My son. But the cowardly, unbelieving, abominable, murderers, sexually immoral, sorcerers, idolaters, and all liars shall have their part in the lake which burns with fire and brimstone, which is the second death."

We can see that checking-out is just as much of a decision as overcoming. In a futurist society that is suddenly without electricity, when someone is tempted to head in a negative direction, their downfall will be quick. You cannot allow disbelief of the situation, no matter how overwhelming, turn into checking out. In times of struggle we must lean into God and refuse to worry about tomorrow, but be fully in the moment.

I'm reminded of a story of a German soldier who was taken prisoner by the Soviets, after the WWII battle of Stalingrad. The German's food supply was so dire before the surrender that a soldier was only given 100gm., none for the wounded or non-fighting. The Soviets had revenge on their minds and had no mercy for those Germans. The prisoners that didn't freeze to death on the long walk were stuffed into box cars that chugged slowly across the endless vastness. Then the prisoners were indiscriminately shot at when the box cars came to a stop. Somewhere in this horrifying plight, a German solder said to himself, "I'm going to live." Not long after, he was shot. Interestingly, 110,000 prisoners were taken, about 5,000 came home, and he was one of them.

HITTING THE PEAK

After hitting the peak there is only one place to go. They say peak-oil has passed; this nation has been drilled up like Swiss cheese. They also say that the human reproduction rate has topped in many parts of the globe. World population growth rate reached its peak above 2% in the 1960's. Since then there's been a surprising drop in fertility rates. The total fertility rate, TFR, is the average number of children women will have in each country. China is down to 1.6, well below replacement. Europe, Russia, Japan, Brazil, Canada, Australia among others are going backwards. The US is barely holding its own. Without immigration some of these nations wouldn't be holding their own. Amazingly the biggest drops have happened in Kuwait, Libya, Maldives, Qatar, and Bangladesh. It is as if people don't have time or money for children anymore.

I recall a trip to the Yucatan, Mexico back in the seventies. We had dinner in a hut, and there were kids running everywhere. I bet the family had six or more. We went back 30 years later, and I ended up talking to a waiter at a restaurant. He was a millennial.

"You married?"

"Yeah."

"How many kids do you have?"

"One."

"Are you going to have more?"

"I'm not sure."

"It's funny, the last time I was down here there were kids running all over the place, people were having kids left and right. Now, you only have one. What happened?"

"I've seen American TV."

I mention this shift in world population because of the mindset of the devil. His mission to kill, steal and destroy. His main goal is to keep as many people from entering the kingdom of God as possible. With death and destruction in his veins, why not hit the earth with WWIII as it is peaking, topping out?

Will this be the time where 2 Thes.:7 plays out and God removes His protective hand? For the mystery of lawlessness is already at work; only He who now restrains will do so until He is taken out of the way.

I believe this entire drama could be the perfect storm in setting up a new world leader. Could the millennials be vulnerable to his beliefs, putty in his hand? And if he's has the power to get electricity flowing again, then look out.

Preemptive Strike

Trump's meeting with China's Xi Jinping in Mar-a-Lago, Florida, looked promising, regarding a North Korean resolution. US. Secretary of State Rex Tillerson commented, ". . . very frank discussion over North Korea."

At that time we thought China would deal with North Korea's nuclear program since they do the lion's share of trade with them. By ratcheting up sanctions on Pyongyang regime, it might shut the program down. But this hasn't been the case.

Lately, our president has tweeted, "Caught RED HANDED – very disappointed that China is allowing oil to go into North Korea. There will never be a friendly solution to the North Korea problem if this continues to happen!"

So, how do you deal with a character like Kim Jong Un who is described by some as a Caligula, a despot?

If there is hope of preventing a strike on our electrical grid, I believe it is in the spiritual realm. Pray to God this cup would pass. On the physical level, Trump is the only president that I've seen in a while that could actually hit North Korea with a preemptive strike and negotiate his way out of it.

For those thinking that the US military can intercept an intercontinental missile, this morning, Feb. 02, 2018, I read that the Aegirs Ashore system failed at intercepting a missile in a test. This was the second unsuccessful attempt in less than a year.

Again, we need to pray.

NOTES

US Balistic Missile Intercept Test Fails for 2nd Time, Franz-Stefan Gady, The Diplomat, Feb. 02, 2018

CONCLUSION

In a world of wars, famines, disease, suicide bombing, persecution, economic turmoil, and natural disasters, how should we live? Fear is a natural response but Christ doesn't want us to panic. He wants us to walk in peace, live fearlessly. We aren't victims but victors. Our mission should be to do His will, and our overwhelming hope should be in Christ's return.

I don't run around all worked up, worried about the future. My future is secure in Christ; He's paid for me and my sins. I don't pretend that these world threats will go away, but plan for the future and prepare accordingly, within my means. But I am not freaked out about any future events. In fact, I do my best to enjoy the good times. As a writer, I'm always praying to get the story out that I believe God wants me write.

I said all that to say, "I hope this book inspires you to prepare."

Much of life is being spiritually, mentally and physically prepared. Of late Hawaiians received a cell message warning of an inbound missile. The message stated, "This isn't a drill." Though the message was false, it made me wonder what I would do if I had only six minutes to get ready for such an attack. Where would I shelter? Personally,

I liked the drill because it helped me preplan for the event instead of suddenly getting the warning.

For me, one of the saddest verses in the Bible is Rev. 13:7 It was granted to him (Beast) to make war with the saints and to overcome them. And authority was given him over every tribe, tongue, and nation. Unfortunately, this verse doesn't say anything about a long war, but straight-up – overcome them. Could it be that the saints weren't ready and their downfall was quick?

Jonah's message to Nineveh, Jonah 3:4 And Jonah began to enter the city on the first day's walk. Then he cried out and said, "Yet forty days, and Nineveh shall be overthrown!" Forty days was the warning.

Pray tell this *warning* will inspire folks to get ready while the trucks are still rolling. Christians should be the most ready people on the planet. That way we can bless others.

POSTSCRIPT

A. WILL THE RAPTURE SAVE US FROM THIS WAR?

The Left Behind series has sold over 70,000,000 copies. Obviously a great number of Christians in this country believe they are going to be beamed-up, taken off the planet before it gets hot. The doctrine goes well with the comfort-prosperity Gospel which is huge in this country.

On TV, some big named preachers, are bellowing out, "You better be ready for the End Times because the rapture is coming."

The initial rapture concept was introduced by a preacher, John Darby, in 1830. It was further popularized during the start of the 20th century by footnotes in the Scofield Reference Bible. Theologians took it from there.

Historically the church believed in the post-tribulation rapture and these days only English speaking people buy into the concept of a pre-tribulation rapture. Foreign Christians consider the doctrine a fairytale, comic bookish. Understandingly as they are getting martyred at an unprecedented rate and there's been no beam-me-up for them prior to being murdered. According to the Center for the Study of Global Christianity, an academic research center that monitors worldwide demographic trends in Christianity, between the years 2004 and 2015, 900,000 Christians were martyred, an average of 90,0000 Christians each year.

End Time martyrs are confirmed by John in his account in Revelation 6:10. When Christ's disciples ask him what it will be like in the End Times, he answers, Matt. 24:9 "Then they will deliver you up to tribulation and kill you, and you will be hated by all nations for my name sake."

I believe in the post-tribulation doctrine because of a number of scriptures. If you are a pre-tribber or mid-tribber, I hope my arguments don't alienate you, I'm sure you are passionate about your belief; my goal here is to prepare the church, not to alienate.

If I were to argue the post-tribulation doctrine I would start with Rev. 22: 18, 19. 'For I testify to everyone who hears the words of the prophecy of this book: If anyone adds to these things, God will add to him the plagues that are written in this book; and if anyone takes away from the words of this prophecy, God shall take away his part from the Book of Life, from the holy city, and from the things which are written in this book.' These verses invoke fear and I don't take them lightly. Nor do I claim to know the date of Christ's return but I do believe the rapture will come on the last trumpet as it says in 1Corinthians 15:51, 52 'Behold, I tell you a mystery: We shall not all sleep, but we shall all be changed in a moment, in the twinkling of an eye, at the last trumpet."

The *seals* in Revelation come before the trumpets. The six seals are hellacious events that, if you are somehow fortunate enough to make it through that time, then you get the seven Trumpets which are more hellacious events.

Revelation 13:7 says, 'It was granted to him to make war with the saints and to overcome them.' So how can the saints be gone prior to the Beast making war on them?"

This is also confirmed in 2 Thessalonians 2:3 'Let no man deceive you by any means: that Day will not come unless the falling away comes first, and the man of sin is revealed.' In other words, the Day of Christ won't come till after the Beast.

The rapture and the second coming of Christ are one and the same. He doesn't return twice. The only way for that to work is to add words to Revelation and we don't want to do that.

Mathew 24:40 and 41 tell us about the rapture, 'Two men will be in the field: one will be taken and the other left. Two women will be grinding at the mill: one will be taken and the other left.' That is the rapture. They will be taken up, caught up off this earth.' Also 1Thessalonians 4:17 tells us, 'Then we who are alive and remain shall be caught up together with them in the clouds to meet the Lord in the air. And thus we shall always be with the Lord.' That is the rapture.

"Mathew 24: 29 and 30 read, "Immediately *after* the tribulation of those days the sun will be darkened, and the moon will not give its light; the stars will fall from heaven, and the powers of the heavens will be shaken. Then the sign of the Son of Man will appear in heaven, and then all tribes of the earth will mourn, and they will see the Son of Man coming on the clouds of heaven with power and great glory.

So you can see his return is clearly stated – after the tribulation of those days. What is perplexing is that so many are preaching two returns of Christ; one rapture before the great tribulation, then another catching up when even the dead get caught up, after the great tribulation, when Christ returns again.

Paul, the apostle, gives the order of how the believers

are caught up on Christ's one and only return in 1 Thessalonians 4: 15, 16, 17, 'For this we say to you by the word of the Lord, that we who are alive and remain until the coming of the Lord will by no means precede those who are asleep. For the Lord Himself will descend from heaven with a shout, with the voice of an archangel, and with the trumpet of God. And the dead in Christ will rise first. Then we who are alive and remain shall be caught up together with them in the clouds to meet the Lord in the air. And thus we shall always be with the Lord.' So this is very clear that the dead will rise first then those who remain will be caught up.

For those who say God doesn't want any of his children to suffer wrath and that is the reason they don't go through the tribulation, I would suggest you consider the Christians that have been recently martyred in the Middle East.

Overseas, Christians are getting killed at an unprecedented rate. The National Religious Broadcasting, NRB, president, Dr. Jerry Johnson, says Christians face genocide in the Middle East. "At the beginning of the Syrian Civil War seven years ago, there were approximately 2.5 million Christians in the country. We are certainly under half of that now. In Iraq, you had about 1.5 million before 2003 and we're at one-fifth of that now, maybe less than that."

Also, could it be that some are taking the scripture on *wrath* out of context? 1 Thes. 5:9 'For God doesn't appoint us to wrath, but to obtain salvation through our Lord Jesus Christ,' The wrath Paul is talking about there is Hell and Damnation, not the great tribulation.

No doubt Revelation is difficult to understand but it does give a certain order of events, often stating, 'after these things.' We know the trumpets are after the seals. Those hellacious events are so intense that Jesus says, Mathew 24:22-22, "For then there will be great tribulation, such as has not been since the beginning of the world until this time, no, nor ever shall be. And unless those days were shortened, no flesh would be saved; but for the elect's sake those days will be shortened." His words prove a post-tribulation catching up or rapture because he mentions, 'except for the elects sake,' so Christians will go through it.

The pre-tribulation doctrine paints the picture of a lovey-dovey god that wouldn't allow His people to remain in harm's way yet that hasn't been the case in real life. Christians were here in WWI, WWII and presently they're getting persecuted like never before. And in Revelation when those saints are calling out for Him to take revenge on their deaths during the great tribulation, God's answer, Revelation 6:11, 'Then a white robe was given to each of them: and it was said to them that they should rest a little while longer, until both the number of their fellow servants and their brethren, who would be killed as they were, was completed.' So, if you examine His answer, there is nothing that is lovey-dovey on the treatment of their fellow servants. They are going to be martyred too. In other words, persecution has happened, is ongoing, is absolutely coming, and God has numbered the Christians that will be martyred. Furthermore, we clearly see that the martyrs came out of the Great Tribulation.

"In Daniel 12: 7, Daniel is told how it is all going to end. ". . . when the power of the holy people is completely shattered . . ." Now consider, if you are one of those holy people during that time, does getting – *completely shattered* – sound like fun? It will be difficult, but there is a martyr's reward on heaven's side and it will all be worth it.

I believe Christians should be prepared. Revelation tells us that during the End Times, one will not be able to buy or sell without the mark of the Beast. So either you prepare for it, line up with the Beast, or starve.

I recall an interview on TV with a Russian Christian who said she was getting mentally ready for another round of persecution. It goes to show how important it is to be ready. This mindset is comparable with the instruction in the Bible of the ten virgins who had oil in their lamps. Interestingly, the instruction is given to the ones with oil not to give theirs up while waiting for the bridegroom. I frown at the thought of what the unprepared will do when chaos rules. Won't they be like the virgins who are caught with no oil in their lamp? That is exactly where the devil would have them.

Expectations are critical in life, which is part of the problem with the prosperity, pre-trib Gospel. They expect to get paid back. People who put money into a pension plan expect to be rewarded with a retirement check. If and when it doesn't play out that way, if and when inflation eats up that pay check, if and when your church dies, life turns sour and God gets the stiff arm.

B. Posterity viewing our generation

Someday we will be history and a future generation will look back on this nation, and try to figure out what led up to this war. What will they see?

1. How has our nation treated Israel?

God promises in Gen. 12:3 to bless those who bless Israel but curse those who slight Israel. If you know the history leading up to Israel's Six Day War with Egypt, Syria and Jordan closing in on them, you know that Israel reacted out of self defense and is entitled to every square foot of land they conquered. The peace agreement at the end of that war was green line ownership of the land conquered. But since 1967 they have given back over 90% of that land.

The UN and American presidents have pressured them to do so. *Land for peace policy* from Carter, Clinton, Bush to Obama, held that Israel's settlements were illegal.

Additionally the UN is a strong mouthpiece against Israel. They have a history of bias against them. During the last confrontation in Gaza, 2014, it wasn't surprising that Hamas missiles were found in three UN schools. The UN is also silent on the genocide of Christians in the Middle East. And the US supports the UN.

As a whole, Millennials have bought into the poor-me, view of the Palestinians in that region and are anti Israel.

2. WHAT HAPPENED TO THIS NATION'S INCARCERATIONS?

According to The National Academies Press - *In 1972, 162 US residents were incarcerated in prisons and jails per 100,000 population: by 2007, that rate had more than quintupled to a peak of 767 per 100,000.*

As far as laws that lead to jail time, America has the highest incarceration rate and the largest total prison population in the entire world by a wide margin.

3. WHAT HAPPENED TO RELIGIOUS AFFILIATION IN OUR NATION?

John Adams, our second President, once said, *"Religion and virtue are the only foundations of all free governments."*

For the most part, in this country, the church is dying.

Note the color of hair when you go into a church these days. If you think attendance is low now, it is being projected that the percentage of Americans attending church in 2050 will be about half of what it is today.

A study conducted by the Barna Group discovered that nearly 60 percent of all Christians from 15 years of age to 29 years of age are no longer actively involved in any church.

In 1972, only 7 percent of all US adults had no religious affiliation. In 1990, 86 percent of Americans identified themselves as "Christian" of one type or another. Today, the younger you are, the greater that number has grown; 32% of all US adults under the age of 30 have no religious affiliation. According to the US Census Bureau, the number of Americans with "No Religion" more than doubled between 1990 and 2008.

4. WHAT HAPPENED TO OUR MILITARY?

Under the Obama administration, they've strategically removed Christians in leadership.

I was told by a friend, "Why would a Christian hang in there when they will not elevate you in rank?"

The results of the lack of Christian leadership can be found in the number of sexual assaults in the military, 20,300 in 2014. The majority of them are male on male. Additionally, the number of active members of the US military killing themselves each year now exceeds the numbers who die on the battlefield.

5. What happened to the use of drugs in America?

In America today there are 60 million people that abuse alcohol and 22 million that use illegal drugs. According to a study conducted by the Mayo Clinic Proceedings, 20 percent of all Americans are on at least five prescription drugs.

According to the Centers for Disease Control and Prevention, doctors in the US write more than 250 million prescriptions for antidepressants each year. Children in the US are three times more likely to be prescribed antidepressants than children in Europe. In the US today, prescription painkillers kill more Americans than heroin and cocaine combined. According to a report from The Council of Economic Advisers, the economic cost of the opioid crisis in 2015 was $504 billion. Its prescriptions play out in a 30 day supply for every American. There are 70 million Americans that are on mind-altering drugs of one form or another. Over half of Americans that are at least 60 years old say they have taken at least one prescription drug within the last month.

Presently the US has the highest rate of illegal drug use on the entire planet.

6. What has happened to American savings?

According to a report from *Time*, nearly half of Americans live paycheck to paycheck. The recession ravaged American's credit scores and now 56% have subprime credit.

7. WHAT HAPPENED TO RELATIONSHIPS IN THIS COUNTRY?

The US has the highest teen pregnancy rate in the entire industrialized world.

According to the Centers for Disease Control and Prevention, one third of the entire population of America has a sexually transmitted disease. That's over 110 million people. It costs our nation over 16 billion a year to treat STDs.

8. WHAT HAPPENED TO OUR FOOD?

Genetically Modified Organisms, GMO, were just underway in 1985. Even though there have been no long term studies on its negative effect, it now is well into our foods. According to NON-GMO Project, *most GMO's have been engineered to withstand the direct application of herbicide. Roundup use has increased fifteen fold since GMO's were first introduced. A growing body of evidence connects GMO's with health problems, environmental damage, and violation of farmers' and consumer's rights. Globally, there are 300 regions with outright bans on growing GMO's.*

Could GMO's have helped turn the US into the most obese country in the world?

9. WHAT HAPPENED TO PRIVACY IN THE US?

The internet has categorized us. Facebook and Twitter sells our information to data miners. You look at an item for purchase on one website then check your email later and you'll notice advertisements for competing items. The same algorithms play out with the articles you read. They know if you are a conservative or liberal, what religion you serve and even what level of commitment.

If Hitler and his SS were in power today, they would drool over what our government knows about us.

On the physical level, perhaps the greatest invasion of privacy comes in the form of SWAT teams. In 1980 there were 3,000 deployments, today over 80,000 raids a year. Most are drug related and involve forcible entry. According to an ACLU report, *65 percent of the raids result in forced entry, battering ram, or some sort of explosive device. Yet in over half of those raids, the police failed to find any sort of weapon.*

10. WHAT HAPPENED TO MARRIAGE IN THIS COUNTRY?

Federal judges will really be remembered by what they did with one of the most sacred institutions we have, marriage. They've dirtied up the most fundamental institution between a man and woman.

Presently America has the highest divorce rate in the world by a good margin.

Back in 1960, 72 percent of adults were married. According to the Pew Research Center, only 51 percent of all American adults are currently married. Christian divorce rate is as bad as non-Christian. Part of the devastating result is one out of every three children in the US lives in a home without a father. The homosexual lobby has pushed into to schools so strongly that some kids these days don't know if they are, boy, girl, or transgender.

11. WHAT HAS HAPPENED TO THE POLITICAL MINDSET?

These days 44% of American millennials would prefer socialism over capitalism. Once it goes over 50%, what will these socialist think of the wealthy? Will they consider those hard working, job creators, evil?

In the 1970's, one of every 50 Americans was on food stamps. Today, it's approximately one of every 6.

12. WHAT HAPPENED WITH OUR NATION'S DEFICIT?

In 1985 our deficit was approximately, 1.5 trillion. Today it is over 20 trillion, not including the unfunded obligations to Social Security, Medicare, and Medicaid. Add on hidden debt and this nation is well over 100 trillion.

In 1985 our nation's debt to GDP was 36%, today is over 100%. A lot of economists are saying, "Default is inevitable at this point."

13. WHAT HAPPENED TO GOVERNMENT ACCOUNTABILITY?

A 2013 Reuters story estimated since 1996 there was 8.5 trillion dollars that was unaccounted for the Pentagon alone. Last year, the Pentagon reported unaccounted figures of 6.5 trillion for just the Army.

According to Mark Skidmore, an economist from Michigan State, and Catherine Fitts, a former assistant secretary of Housing and Urban Development, between the years 1998-2015, total missing money for HUD and the Pentagon is $21 trillion.

14. What happened to technology in this nation?

Where does one start with that one? Much of what we have today would be considered Sci-Fi in 1985. From drones to facial recognition to electric cars, surveillance cameras, digital reality, artificial intelligence, smart phones and computers, we've come a long way.

Radio-frequency identification, RFID, microchip technologies have gone well past holding our medical records, or building access and security. They are common implants for pets, tracking their location. They are also on our credit cards, tracking our location. Scientist used to pride themselves about getting RFID down to the size of a grain of rice, but now they are so tiny they can be shot in to the blood with a needle. Via a flu shot?

15. What happened to the mindset of Christians in this nation?

Here are some of Barna.com's notable findings among practicing Christians.

- 61% agree with ideas rooted in New Spirituality
- 54% resonate with postmodernist views (postmodernist advances the idea that there is no such thing as objectivity).
- 36% accept ideas associated with Marxism
- 29% believe ideas based on secularism

Brooke Hempell, senior vice president of research for Barma says, "This research really crystallizes what Barna has been tracking in our country as an ongoing shift away from Christianity as the basis for a shared worldview.

We have observed and reported on increasing pluralism, relativism and moral decline among Americans and even in the Church. Nevertheless, it is striking how pervasive some of these beliefs are among people who are actively engaged in the Christian faith."

Coming from an OmniPoll conducted in an online study, they conclude – only 17% of practicing Christians have a biblical worldview.

16. What's happened to cash?

Of late, China and Russia have come to terms over trading oil without the use of the mighty US dollar. This agreement is a blast over the bow to the petrodollar agreement that was set up by Secretary of State, Henry Kissinger, with Saudi Arabia in 1974, where the Saudis priced oil in US dollars and in return the House of Saud got our protection from rebels and invaders. U.S. dollars represent nearly 100% of global oil sales, and the boat starts rocking when China and Russia propose to bypass the dollar in trade with the rest of the BRIC nations. Is this the beginning of the end of our dollar?

The banking/globalist play it as if cash were evil, showing pictures of piles of cash that drug lords possess. Presently the International Monetary Fund, IMF, is engineering a new financial system, a different ledger system, which shifts away from the mighty US dollar.

These moves may seem of no consequence to most people, but our leaders know they are huge. It wasn't long after Saddam Hussein said he was going to trade his oil for Euros when his government buildings were struck by our missiles. Additionally, before Gaddafi died, he was trying to introduce African currency linked to gold. Some say the gold Dinar would have thrown the world's economy into chaos. Who says wars are started over ideologies?

It's not hard to imagine a very large terrorist event being the precursor to a cashless society. If and when that comes about, what will happen to your bank account if you don't line up with the thought patterns of the Beast?

17. WHAT HAS HAPPENED TO OUR PUBLIC SCHOOL?

Much has changed since they took Bible reading out of public schools in the early 60's. For the most part, God has been told He's not welcome in our public schools, "Don't come around here no more." Does this new generation even know that Christ suffered and died on a cross for them; that God's has an amazing plan for their lives? And how do they determine their moral standards?

These days' metropolitan teachers will point out any ills done to any religion except Christianity. In classrooms across the country, teachers preach the religion of evolution, one species evolving into another like its fact, even though real science proves macro-evolution is impossible, a lie. Our kids are getting brainwashed at an early age with kindergarten teachers handing out pictures of dinosaurs, claiming they evolved and walked the earth 50 million years ago.

According to a recent Pew Research survey, 60 percent of all Americans believe, "humans and other living things have evolved over time."

The end-all of that message – God had nothing to do with creation, and the individual is just an animal with no purpose whatsoever. One result of this is a godless generation. Another result is poor SAT scores; none to brag about, they have been falling for years. At this point, 15-year-olds who attend US public schools do not even rank in the top half of all industrialized nations when it comes to math or science literacy.

18. WHAT HAPPENED TO THE MEDIA IN THIS NATION?

These days the press has come out from the veil and showed itself as quite the liberal mouthpiece; anything conservative, anything Christian, they relentlessly poo-poo. Did you notice there was no honeymoon for Trump when he became president, no seven month grace? Their attacks on him were violent, even promoting people who wanted to murder him.

Interestingly, it doesn't matter how much crud they print, people read it. Fake news abounds for a reason.

19. WHAT HAPPENED TO THE KILLING OF INNOCENTS IN THIS NATION?

Since Roe v. Wade over 50 million babies have been slaughtered in this country. And not just killed but cut up for body parts and sold. The number of American babies killed by abortion each year is roughly equal to the number of US military deaths that have occurred in all of the wars the US has ever been involved in combined. The US has the highest abortion rate in the western world.

20. WHAT HAPPENED TO AMERICAN ENTERTAINMENT?

In 1983 the internet was born. Who knew then how powerful a communications network it would turn into? Now an astonishing 30 percent of all internet traffic goes to adult websites. Seventy percent of young men visit at least one adult website every month. The average high school boy spends two hours on adult websites every single week. It has been estimated that 89 percent of all pornography is produced in the US.

Virtual reality and artificial intelligence will create an experience for them that's tough to compete against in real life. If a woman's married to someone addicted to porn, she'll feel degraded. This is the devil's entry to destroy the marriage, to destroy the family.

In 1985 video games were nothing like what we see today. Now, according to the National Center for Education Statistics, young Americans will spend 10,000 hours playing video games before the age of 21. That's twice the time it takes to earn a bachelor's degree.

Most of these games are violent. When it's played out on real streets and blood flows, everyone stands around gaping, and can't figure out why. In the end, guns are blamed, not the evil.

If someone from the 1950's saw what we have on TV now wouldn't they think we were living in the Last Days? Have we been desensitized?

21. What's happened to preaching in this country?

The following churches have now allowed lesbians into their *leadership* - United Methodist, Episcopal Church, Evangelical Lutheran Church in America, Presbyterian Church, (U.S.A.) Unitarian Universalist Association of Churches, United Church of Christ.

It has to be disheartening for the men and women who spent countless years plowing the soil, only to hand the churches off to the next generation who have taken them opposite to Biblical teaching.

The good news is our pastors are still free to preach the Gospel. It's great to hear them on TV saying, "We are new creatures in Christ. He's paid for our sin and Heaven isn't attained by our works but by Christ's work on the cross."

I don't know what it is, but sometimes it's hard to see these new creatures living out the Gospel in today's society. Just down the road a pastor was replaced because he was getting a divorce. He was replaced by a woman minister who condoned lesbians in that church's leadership.

These aren't the days where pastors speak of hell fire and brimstone like they did in the 1800's. Lately, I heard a big name TV preacher near mockingly asking those who go there, "How's that going for you?"

Today, a lot of the Gospel message that goes out proclaims that we are free from the law and never mentions the word, 'sin.' Additionally, the law is looked at as a bad thing, a cursed thing. Some have a doctrine that once you initially repent; you don't have to repent again, period. And a lot of the Gospel that goes out presents no cost on our side.

There's little talk of taking up your cross and following Christ but lots of talk on how to look after your feelings, how to get your Cadillac's, how to attain *your* dreams – plant your seed money here.

This god that some preachers have created is so lovey dovey, so full of grace, that he won't cast anyone into hell. The god they have created is some kissy, kissy god that is so full of love that he can literally go against his own rules. This teaching has spawned a void of the fear of God.

Who preaches God's other characteristics besides just love, mercy and grace? Where is the God of fierceness and judgment, the jealous God of anger and wrath, the God of all power and might, the God of creativity and imagination, the God of wisdom, order and His word, the God of shepherding, law, rules, boundaries and righteousness, the God of vastness and space, the God of healing, understanding, restoration and peace, the God of dance, intimacy and romance, the God of provision and compassion, the God of presence, relationships and sorrow, the God of unsearchable mystery, joy and truth, the God of strategy, targets and war, the God whose robe is dipped in blood and will rule with a rod of iron?

Could we be the lukewarm church which has fallen into the flow of culture and is best explained in Revelation 3:17 Because you say, 'I am rich, have become wealthy, have need of nothing' – and do not know that you are wretched, miserable, poor, blind and naked –.

Thank God for the selfless humble evangelists, prophets, and pastors that are tuned into Christ, tuned into his Holy Spirit, look after their flock, and carry the torch of the *entire* Gospel. It's great to hear them preach, "Take up your cross and follow me." These days, they have their work cut out for them.

May God continue to bless them!

22. WHAT HAS HAPPENED WITH BIG BROTHER?

Deep State has taken control of the system, through your laptop they can hear your conversation in a room, they have access to your emails, they know what you look at on the internet, they record everything you say on your phone, they know what you buy on your credit cards, they know what programs you're watching on TV, your GPS on your cell phone will tell them where you are, and from the

Persistent Surveillance System, they can record where you travel.

Do you sense them reading your e-mails?

23. What's happened with terrorism in this country?

Muslim terrorist actions on 9/11 truly brought them to light. These days we are seeing more and more non-Muslim extremist. Recently there was the Las Vegas shooter who killed 59 at a concert, another in Texas that killed 22 at a church and another school shooting in Florida that killed 17.

It is terrible to simply give out the number of dead when these individuals have names and were connected to love ones.

24. What's happened to language in our country?

Remember when gay used to mean gay? Remember when the rainbow sign used to refer to God's promises to earth? What did tolerate used to mean? Remember when BC used to mean Before Christ and AD meant after His death. Now it's BCE, before the common era.

It's as if the devil has turned language upside down, hijacked it. Even with abortion, the liberals are called pro-choice and the conservatives are called anti-abortion. So Christians are tagged anti's and if you make waves in the liberal arena then you are tagged a hate monger.

And how about political correctness? Isn't it a subtle way of saying, "If you aren't thinking our way, our mindset, in line with our socialist politics, then you are not just off the wall but really out-there?"

What's ironic is the socialist mindset is one of the least tolerant mindsets on the planet. They praise diversity but have no tolerance for Christians. Check out the Marxist killing/murdering record to see what they've done with those who don't line up with their politics. Thiers is a totalitarian mindset.

Can you see the slippery slope of this nation?

Can you see this nation has planted some nasty seeds?

Do you see a day of reckoning coming?

Can you see this nation flying in a hellacious snow storm, struggling to stay in the air as it sweeps toward a granite mountain?

Pray that North Americans start to fear almighty God.

NOTES

20 missiles found in UN-run school in Gaza, Raphael Ahren, The Times of Israel, 17 July, 2014

U. N. silent during ISIS genocide of Christians, Michael Haverluck (OneNewsNow.com) Feb. 15, 2017

Crime, Prisoners, Per Capita: Countries Compared Data for 2003 Number prisoners held per 100,000 population, nationmaster.com

ARIS 2013 Team, Press: Generation X Becoming Less Christian, Less Republican; Catholic and Baptist Losses Feed Religious Polarization, May 31, 2013 americanreligionsurvey.-aris.org

Michael Snyder, Sexual Assaults in The Military Are At An All-time High And Most of Them Are Male on Male, March 17, 2014, endofamericandream.com, paragraph 1

Pg. 124 David Kupelian, 70 Million Americans Taking Mind-Altering Drugs, Feb 9, 2014, worldnetdaily.com, paragraph 3= alcohol, paragraph8= drugs

Americans Take Prescription Drugs, June 19, 2013 Mayo Clinic, Olmsted Medical Center Find, newsnetwork. mayoclinic.org, paragraph 2

U.S. Leads the World in Illegal Drug Use, Jennifer Warner, WebMD, July 1, 2008

Nearly Half of America Lives Paycheck-to-Paycheck, Christopher Matthews, Time, Jan 30, 2014

Why is the teen birth rate in the United States so high and why does it matter?, Kearney MS, Levine PB, J Econ Perspect., NCBI, 2012 Spring:26(2):141-66

The Excessive Militarization of American Policing, ACLU, April 17, 2015

Ian Graham, People Divorce rate: Countries Compared, Feb 27, 2005, nationmaster.com

Carol Morello, Married Couples at a Record Low, Dec 14, 2011, washingtonpost.com

Luke Rosiak, Fathers disappear from households across America, Dec.25, 2012

Poll: Nearly Half of Millennials Prefer Socialism to Capitalism, Bre Payton, the Federalist, Nov. 1, 2017

Food stamp use reaches another high in September: 47.7 million participants, Caroline May, The Daily Caller, 12/09/2012

Pentagon's Sloppy Bookkeeping Means 6.5 Trillion Can't Pass an Audit, Eric Pianin, The Fiscal Times

Has Our Government Spent $21 Trillion Of Our Money Without Telling Us?, Laurence Kotlikoff, Forbes, Dec 8, 2017

Polling and Analysis, "Nones" on the Rise, Pews Research Center, Oct. 9 2012

Polling and Analysis, Public's Views on Human Evolution, Dec 30, 2013, Pew Research Center, pewforum.org

Digest of Education Statistics, National Center for Education Statistics nces.ed.gov/programs/digest/d08/tables/dt08

Randy O'Bannon, 56,662,169 Abortions in America Since Roe vs. Wade in 1973, lifenews.com, Jan 12, 2014

Ted Thornhill, Is the whole world looking at porn? Biggest site goes over Four Billion hits a month. April 9, 2017 "in the paper" Daily Mail.com under Science and Tech

David Roach, Pastors say Porn Impacts Their Churches, Many unsure What to Do. Nov 10, 2011, www. Lifeway.com (paragraph 8)

Ashley Lutz, Porn and Video Games are Ruining the Next Generation of American Men, June 1, 2012, businessinsider.com

Michael Arrington, Internet Pornography Stats, May 12, 2007, techcrunch.com

Michael Snyder - The American Dream, Fighting to Restore Our Constitutional Republic

Acknowledgements

I'd like to thank my wife, Elaine, for her editing and critiquing. Special thanks going out to Rod and Linda Allen, Joseph Schmalenbach, for their kind but honest critiquing. I'm so very fortunate to have you as friends.

This book wouldn't be what it is without their efforts. Thank you all so much.

Made in the USA
San Bernardino, CA
13 February 2019